T0265575

CATCHING EXCELLENCE

CATCHING EXCELLENCE

THE HISTORY OF THE GREEN BAY PACKERS IN ELEVEN GAMES

CHUCK CARLSON

LYONS
PRESS

Essex, Connecticut

An imprint of Globe Pequot, the trade division of
The Rowman & Littlefield Publishing Group, Inc.
4501 Forbes Blvd., Ste. 200
Lanham, MD 20706
www.rowman.com

Distributed by NATIONAL BOOK NETWORK

British Library Cataloguing in Publication Information Available

Library of Congress Cataloging-in-Publication Data Available

ISBN 978-1-4930-6284-3 (cloth : alk. paper)
ISBN 978-1-4930-6913-2 (electronic)

♾️™ The paper used in this publication meets the minimum requirements of American National
Standard for Information Sciences—Permanence of Paper for Printed Library Materials, ANSI/
NISO Z39.48-1992.

CONTENTS

CONTENTS

FOREWORD

BY RON WOLF

I STILL REMEMBER VIVIDLY AND FONDLY WHAT I CONSIDER PERHAPS the greatest game in my 10 years as the Green Bay Packers' executive vice president and general manager.

And it may not be the one you think it is. Obviously, there have been a lot of great games played by this remarkable franchise. And in my time there, from 1991 to 2001, I witnessed a lot.

But for me the pinnacle came on a cold, sunny afternoon at Lambeau Field when I saw the historic old stadium that I had grown to love shake in ways I didn't know it could shake.

The seconds were ticking off the scoreboard, the sellout crowd was screaming, and I'm watching the players, many of whom I had brought to the team over the previous seasons, celebrating and hugging and laughing and, yes, crying.

This was a big deal. On this January afternoon in 1997, I watched as the Green Bay Packers defeated the Carolina Panthers to win the NFC championship and earn Green Bay's first trip back to the Super Bowl in 30 years.

The Packers would go on to win Super Bowl XXXI in New Orleans, beating the New England Patriots, and afterward, when Mike Holmgren told his team that as important as winning the Vince Lombardi Trophy was to every other team in the NFL, it meant more to Green Bay, I smiled. He was right.

I think I can say that anybody who has ever played for the Green Bay Packers has been proud to do so. It is a franchise built on tradition and excellence. This is a special team and a special place.

I have often thought back to 1991, when I had the opportunity to join the Packers. I was certainly tempted, but I knew the Packers had struggled for years, and when I sought advice from friends and NFL colleagues about joining the Packers, they cautioned against it. It would be a dead-end job, they said, that would bring nothing but frustration and disappointment.

But when Packers President Bob Harlan told me that I would be in charge of all aspects of football operations, I was intrigued and flattered. I saw it as a great challenge.

So I said yes, and it was the best decision I ever made.

With the help of a lot of people, we were able to do some great work in Green Bay because, let's face it, we resurrected a franchise that wasn't really going anywhere. In fact, there were rumors for years that the Packers were headed to Milwaukee, but, as I'm sure most football fans know, to have the Packers anywhere else but Green Bay just didn't make sense.

I was very fortunate because you can't have a better situation than being able to work for the Green Bay Packers. It's about their history and what they mean to professional football and just how unique the franchise is. Everything about it is unique. The uniqueness of the city, the uniqueness of the team. And I think we took that uniqueness and made it even more unique.

I also remember when free agency came into the NFL and people said Green Bay would be dead. Guess what? Green Bay is not dead. It had a rebirth, and I'm very proud of what we were able to do to change the dynamic. And, again, it's because of the tradition of the Green Bay Packers.

This book describes some of the most important games in the history of the Packers. It's amazing to see how those games span the decades, proving that great games can come at any time and from players with vastly different skills, perspectives, and goals.

But the games are played by men who have loved the game in ways that few outside the sport can understand. And for me, most of the guys who played for the Packers when I was there have a special place in my heart. For example, I placed my career in the hands of Brett Favre, and he didn't let me down.

So many guys came in and did so well. Two of them, Adam Timmerman and Mark Tauscher, were seventh-round draft picks and played at a championship caliber. Those are the kinds of guys who mean so much to me. They demonstrated so much and showed that if you're good enough, you'll play. And that's the dynamic of the game.

I continue to watch the Packers and am pleased to see that the success and devotion to the game and to the franchise continues under guys like head coach Matt LaFleur, quarterback Aaron Rodgers, general manager Brian Gutekunst, and so many others.

I will always cherish my years with the Green Bay Packers and will always appreciate the opportunity I was provided. We had great players who played great games in front of great fans.

We had a pretty good run up there.

Ron Wolf was executive vice president and general manager of the Green Bay Packers from 1991 to 2001. In his time there, the Packers won one Super Bowl and played in another; posted a .639 overall winning percentage and .841 at home; set a team record with 25 straight wins at Lambeau Field; racked up eight winning seasons; and made the playoffs six times. He was inducted into the Pro Football Hall of Fame in 2015.

INTRODUCTION

It was one of the favorite stories of the late, great Green Bay Packers defensive end Willie Davis, a story that has become one of the many that has been woven into the ever-enlarging fabric of this unique franchise.

It is probably best to first let it be known that to be a Green Bay Packers player, no matter the era, was (and is) to be a storyteller. You almost had no choice; being a part of this group meant not only being a great tactician or athlete but also having the personality of a game-show host.

Whether born to the skill naturally like Curly Lambeau, Paul Hornung, LeRoy Butler, Mike Holmgren, or Aaron Jones, or more reticent types like Reggie White, Mike McCarthy, and Aaron Rodgers, it is a skill learned by all Packers in the roiling cauldron of playing for a team with crushing expectations. Tell great stories and you are part of the family.

Of course, some of those tales were sprinkled with exaggerations and half-truths, but they were always engaging and some were as truthful as passing time and bluster would allow. But they were always fun, usually not suitable for all audiences, and always a way of showing the significance of the team that, for many players, became a second family.

Davis, a Packer for 10 seasons and a member of the Pro Football Hall of Fame, was no different.

He had been traded to the Packers prior to the 1960 season by the Cleveland Browns, who could not find the right place for the athletic Davis to play.

But Davis was stunned and unhappy with the trade because, simply, he did not want to play in the NFL wasteland that was Green Bay,

Wisconsin. Still, he knew it was an opportunity to actually play, so he took a deep breath, put his ego on the shelf, and joined a team that seemed to be making strides under a new and still untested head coach named Vince Lombardi. And he was right.

"The best thing that ever happened to me was coming to Green Bay," Davis said frequently.

Which brings us to our story, or, more accurately, his story. For Davis, it was the perfect encapsulation of who the Packers of the 1960s were and, more important, what they would grow to be.

No one knows how many times he told the story of the 1960 NFL Championship Game between the Packers and the Philadelphia Eagles. But it always brought a smile to his face as well as to all those people who heard the tale—whether it was for the first time or the 500th.

Both the Packers and the Eagles entered that game as something of an anomaly. Only two years earlier, each had resided in the basement of their respective divisions, two franchises mired in mediocrity that, this season, had found redemption in very different ways.

The Packers had hired a volcanic presence as their head coach a year earlier. Vince Lombardi had been a relatively unknown offensive coordinator for the New York Giants who had believed his opportunity to get the one job he craved—head coach—had passed him by.

But the Packers, a franchise going nowhere in a hurry, had tried four head coaches since the legendary Curly Lambeau resigned, and each had been worse than the last.

So the Packers hired Lombardi, and the shrugging of shoulders around Wisconsin and the Packers locker room was thunderous.

"Who the hell is Vince Lombardi?" veteran wide receiver Max McGee said at the time.

He wasn't alone in that sentiment.

The Packers' starting quarterback then, Bart Starr, had struggled under two inefficient and overmatched head coaches in his first three seasons, throwing nearly twice as many interceptions as touchdowns (25 to 13). Worse, the Packers had won just eight games in those three seasons, and the shaken Starr was beginning to wonder if he was even meant for a career in the NFL.

And, of course, he had his own story about his new coach, recalling that his only knowledge of the mercurial New Yorker was from a previous preseason game against the Giants when he watched in amazement as offensive coordinator Lombardi screamed at the Giants defense for poor play.

"I thought, *This guy is crazy*," Starr recalled.

And now he was their head coach.

But in that first season of 1959, Lombardi steered the Packers to a 7–5 mark, their first winning record since 1947 and an amazing improvement from the 1–10–1 disaster of the season before (with roughly the same personnel) under Ray McLean.

In 1960 the improvement continued as the Packers posted an 8–4 record (their best since they won their last NFL championship in 1944) and qualified for the NFL title game.

The Eagles were in a similar state. They had won back-to-back titles in 1948 and 1949 but had done nothing since. In 1959 their fortunes improved, too, finishing 7–5; one year later, under the turbulent leadership of 34-year-old quarterback Norm Van Brocklin, the Eagles rang up a 10–2 record.

So the two teams met for the NFL championship at Philadelphia's Franklin Field. The Packers led 6–0 on two Paul Hornung field goals, but the Eagles claimed the halftime lead, 10–6, thanks in part to Van Brocklin's 35-yard touchdown pass to Tommy McDonald.

A Starr-to-McGee TD pass in the fourth quarter put the Packers back on top, but with five minutes remaining in the game, the Eagles' Ted Dean scored on a five-yard run to again give Philadelphia the lead at 17–13.

In the game's waning minutes, Starr led the Packers back down the field to the Philly 22-yard line. But on what proved to be the game's final play, Starr completed a pass over the middle to fullback Jim Taylor, who was tackled by Eagles All-Pro linebacker Chuck Bednarik at the eight. The crafty Bednarik, who had unretired that season to seek one more championship, kept the struggling Taylor on the ground for the final few precious seconds until the game was over.

"Now you can get up Taylor," Bednarik is reputed to have said. "This f—-ing game is over."

A crowd of 67,000 was on hand to watch the game, and one of the largest TV audiences at that time to ever watch an NFL title game tuned in around the country. And they saw the Packers, for years an NFL afterthought to a growing army of pro football fans, dominate the Eagles, gaining 401 total yards to Philly's 296. Though no one knew it at the time, it would prove to be a Green Bay coming-out party.

Still, after the game the Packers were devastated. They knew they had outplayed the Eagles for most of the game, yet mistakes and perhaps a little uncertainty had cost them in the end. They had finished only eight yards short of a championship, and that would be a tough realization to deal with.

This, of course, was all part of Davis's story, which would then build to a crescendo. He recalled how the coach came into the locker room and looked at his players, who had given so much.

Lombardi's oration was not fiery nor full of empty platitudes of giving your best and leaving it all on the field. He took responsibility for the loss and made a vow.

"He looked at us and told us, 'This is the last championship we lose while I'm the head coach,'" Davis recounted time and again. "That's all he said."

Then Davis would often pause for dramatic effect. "We believed him, too."

The Packers would indeed return, winning titles in 1961 and 1962 and then reeling off three straight championships in 1965, 1966, and 1967, a feat that has yet to be duplicated since in the NFL.

Willie Davis died in April 2020 at age 85, still as devoted to the Green Bay Packers as he was 60 years earlier when he joined a team that, he admits, saved his career.

He always called that loss a great game, especially for what it signaled for the Packers' future.

A great game. We hear that phrase a lot in sports. Great. Memorable. Exciting. Scintillating. Pick an adjective. But was it an important game? Ah, now that's a whole new ballgame, so to speak.

In many ways it was, because of the seeds it planted for a team that would dominate the decade and whose fame would resonate over the years.

But in more than 100 years of playing professional football in Green Bay, is it one of the most important games in team history? Time and circumstances and history seem to suggest no. The Packers have played a lot of meaningful, exciting, crucial games over the years, and many have been chronicled time and time again by those who have watched the NFL overall and the Packers in particular.

This is another opportunity to do that. And with the benefit of hindsight and the viewpoint of many who were there, this is a chance to explore the most important games in this remarkable franchise's history.

It is entirely subjective, of course, but it is also based on criteria that should be taken into account when discussing such a topic. Just to be clear, this list will be done chronologically and not by order of perceived importance. The idea is to focus on games that changed not only the team but the city of Green Bay, the state of Wisconsin, Packers fans from Anchorage to Zanzibar, and, yes, the NFL itself.

As with most of these efforts, there is plenty of room for disagreement and, in an effort to answer those critics and the concerns of everyone who may disagree with the selections, we will also include a few more games that were important but perhaps just fell a little short.

Nonetheless, this book aims to provide a view of some of the matchups that have truly made a difference for this franchise. There will be plenty of context to show that the games being highlighted were not played in a vacuum and, always, there will be stories told and retold about these games—because they live both in history and in the memories of Packers fans.

Hopefully this book will generate some dialogue, spark some memories, and provide an opportunity to think again about special times for a franchise that was born, struggled, thrived, and has now established itself as one of the great, and perhaps indispensable, sports stories in American history.

And in the long run, maybe that's the most important story of all.

CHAPTER ONE

"THE GREATEST FOOTBALL TEAM IN THE WORLD TODAY"

PACKERS 20, NEW YORK GIANTS 6

NOVEMBER 24, 1929

The Packers bring down the Giants' Benny Friedman after a 10-yard gain, separating him from his helmet in the process. AP PHOTO/FILE

THE GREEN BAY PACKERS WERE BORN IN CHAOS, AND FOR THEIR FIRST 10 years, their very existence was in question.

Football had been a part of northeast Wisconsin years before anyone realized the game could be played professionally, and certainly before there was something known as the National Football League.

The still-fledgling game of football was rough, vicious, and dangerous. It had few rules that participants had any interest in paying attention to, and it was a game finding its place in a changing America. This was a country growing in confidence and swagger, and football was a game that reflected that arrogance.

Football teams had popped up all over the place, consisting mostly of local kids who wanted to bang heads with their buddies and then drink beer afterward. Its popularity had grown to the point that it had become a staple on college campuses, evolving into an intercollegiate sport (after warnings from federal officials to establish rules to make the game less dangerous).

And it was no different in northeast Wisconsin, where football had become an obsession for a talented young athlete in Green Bay named Earl Lambeau. Nicknamed "Curly" because of his hair, Lambeau had fallen in love with the brutal simplicity of football, and he played every chance he got.

He was a star athlete at Green Bay East High School, and after graduating in 1917, he had an opportunity to try out for the University of Wisconsin's freshman football team, though he never enrolled in Madison.

Instead, Lambeau went to work for his father's construction company, and in 1918 he caught the eye of perhaps college football's first iconic head coach, the University of Notre Dame's Knute Rockne.

Lambeau made the team, but a severe case of tonsillitis forced him out of school and back home to Green Bay. By the time he recovered, he was ready to move on to other adventures. And first on his list, of course, was football.

In a story that all Packers fans know by heart, Lambeau teamed up with George Whitney Calhoun, editor of the *Green Bay Press-Gazette* newspaper, and with the help of a $500 loan from the Indian Packing Company, where Lambeau had worked as a shipping clerk, Lambeau and Calhoun created the Green Bay football team in 1919. Originally known as the Indians in honor of the packing company, Lambeau was convinced to change the team's name to the Packers—a name he never liked. That's part of the story, too.

And so it started. The story of the Green Bay Packers had begun and, while it was a team that dominated the local competition it played from Wisconsin and the Upper Peninsula of Michigan, chaos was never far behind.

That's because money was always tight, and while the team itself was wildly popular with fans and drew well, their tiny venues—first Hagemeister Park, which was barely more than a pasture, and then 5,000-seat Bellevue Park—could not provide the revenue needed even in 1920s America.

"The Packers were perpetually on their death bed from the day they were born until the 1950 stock sale," said Cliff Christl, a Green Bay native and longtime Packers beat writer for the *Press-Gazette* and *Milwaukee Journal* before becoming the team's official historian in 2014. "For more than 30 years, and probably more than 40, this team was living day by day."

But despite the nearly nonstop financial tribulations that dogged the team off the field, on the field the Packers were as competitive as any team in the ever-evolving league.

Starting with the old American Professional Football League in 1921 (which fielded 21 teams) and then on to the National Football League in 1922, the Packers were a match for teams from big cities like Chicago and New York. And through those formative, difficult years, Lambeau, first as player-coach and later as strictly the head coach, was building a powerhouse.

And in 1929 everything came together. By that season Lambeau had lured some of the game's greatest talent to Green Bay, including linemen like Mike Michalske, Cal Hubbard, and Jug Earp. He brought in a discontented superstar running back in Johnny "Blood" McNally and supplemented it all with great role players such as Lavvie Dilweg, Bo Molenda, Verne Lewellen, and Boob Darling.

That season the NFL was still in its formative, adolescent stage, adding and discarding teams as it became clear which franchises could sustain the level of quality, competitiveness, and, yes, financial stability to succeed in the long run.

So, as the Packers faced teams like the Dayton Triangles, the Frankford Yellow Jackets, and the Providence Steam Roller, they also faced opponents whose names would ring familiar with the future of the NFL: teams like the Chicago Bears, the Chicago Cardinals (who would in time become the St. Louis and Arizona Cardinals), and the New York Giants.

The Giants had joined the NFL in 1925 and already had a championship to their credit in 1927. But they had slipped in 1928, falling to 4–7–2, their first losing season in the league. But they were back in 1929, rolling to an 8–0–1 record and outscoring their foes 204–29 before hosting the Packers in a November 24 game at the Polo Grounds.

Green Bay was also having an epic season, its best since joining the NFL. The Packers came to New York with a 9–0 record and a defense for the ages, having allowed just 16 points while scoring 128.

National interest in the game was intense. Yes, it was clearly a matchup between the game's two best teams, but it was also an irresistible story involving the major metropolis of New York facing the tiny town somewhere in Wisconsin. David vs. Goliath? Sure, why not?

Making it even more entertaining was the fact that the NFL had yet to devise a playoff system to crown a league champion (that wouldn't happen until 1933).

"You could not have had a bigger showdown in terms of what their records were," Christl said. "This was going to be the showdown for the [league] championship."

So on a rainy, cold afternoon, and barely a month after the stock market crash signaled the start of the Great Depression, the Packers dominated the Giants.

Herdis McCrary caught a four-yard touchdown pass from Verne Lewellen in the first quarter, and the defenses dominated for the rest of the half as Green Bay led 7–0.

In the third quarter the Giants closed to within a point when their star, Tony Plansky, caught a 15-yard scoring pass from Benny Friedman. But that was all the Giants could muster.

In the fourth quarter Green Bay back Bo Molenda, whom sportswriters on the scene deemed the star of the game, scored on a one-yard run. Johnny McNally added a three-yard touchdown, and the Packers won 20–6.

The victory sent shock waves through professional football and even impressed the relentlessly cynical New York media.

"Until yesterday it was inconceivable that any football team in the country could defeat the Giants three touchdowns to one," wrote *New York Herald Tribune* sportswriter Rud Rennie. "They have such a powerful team."

Ken Smith of the *New York Graphic* wrote: "The whole blamed team [the Packers] is an all-American eleven, to my mind the greatest football team in the world today."

The Giants rebounded nicely from their first loss, winning their final five games, finishing 13–1–1 and keeping pressure on the Packers to continue winning.

The Packers would sputter the following week, managing just a scoreless tie with the Frankford Yellow Jackets. But the week after that, Green Bay blanked the Providence Steam Roller 25–0, setting up a season finale with the already-hated Chicago Bears that would decide the league championship.

The storied Bears-Packers rivalry didn't just materialize out of thin air or from the imagination of an overwrought sportswriter.

It began, well, at the beginning, when Bears founder and coach George Halas opposed Green Bay's entry into the new National Football League. And though he finally relented, Curly Lambeau never forgot Halas's opposition. From their first meeting in 1921 (won by the Bears 20–0), there has been a special feeling when these two teams meet.

So it was on the final day of the 1929 season when the Bears, far out of contention with a 4–8–2 record, knew they could end a disappointing season by handing the Packers their only loss of the season and denying them a championship.

But it didn't quite work out that way, as the Packers defense intercepted four Bears passes and Eddie Kotal scored two touchdowns on the way to a 25–0 win.

As written by the *Milwaukee Sentinel*: "A crowd of over 5,000 diehards witnessed the game. They came with the expectations of seeing an aroused Bear team humble the champions, but they remained to marvel at the brilliance of the Packers, who were champions in every respect."

The Packers were the first league champs to go through the season without a loss, and the players, if they weren't embraced by the community and the state before, were now treated as heroes. Indeed, on their return from Chicago after clinching the title, more than 20,000 people greeted the team at the train station.

As well, on the day after the pivotal win over the Giants that all but clinched the league title, the *Green Bay Press-Gazette* initiated a "Championship Fund" to reward the players for their performance. Remember, there was no NFL title game at the time and, of course, there was no postseason pay either, as there would be a few years later when a playoff system was installed.

The community responded to the fundraising effort by contributing more than $5,000 in two weeks, and this was with the Great Depression already starting to intensify. At the postseason awards banquet and celebration, each player was awarded $220 and a new watch from the fund as a thank-you.

The late November victory over the Giants was simply the most important game in the young history of the franchise and remains so all these years later. It was a game, and a championship, that was important in so many ways.

"That game kind of sealed them and gave them a national identity," Christl said. "Sports fans in general didn't know about the Packers and now they did. That game was so important in their survival."

Christl said it was also important for the Packers' vital bottom line.

"There's a misconception that the fans saved the Packers," he said. "Green Bay was no different than Canton or any of those other cities that lost NFL franchises. Green Bay wasn't big enough to support an NFL team, but after the 1929 game, the Packers became a favorite drawing card around the league. It was the fans in New York and Chicago who saved the Packers, because they packed the stands at the Polo Grounds and Wrigley Field to watch the Packers. The Packers would go to New York after that and they would draw more than 30,000 fans, and NFL crowds at the time were about 12,000. Gate [receipts] meant everything and teams would share those, so that really helped the Packers financially."

And there was more.

"The '29 game was probably the start of America's romance with the Packers," Christl said. "It put them on the map everywhere. Fans thought for the Packers to go in and knock off a New York team at the Polo Grounds was really something. Thereafter, when the Packers played in New York, they'd practice in Central Park or at Clinton High School [in New York City] and fans would pack the place to watch. And Curly Lambeau was a celebrity. Remember, pro football at the time was a second-class sport, but everything changed after that game in terms of the publicity they received."

With that one game, the Green Bay Packers had forced their way into the public consciousness of an already sports-mad nation. They remain there a century later.

CHAPTER TWO

"AS FINE A SQUAD OF MEN AS EVER REPRESENTED ANY CITY"

PACKERS 21, BOSTON REDSKINS 6

DECEMBER 13, 1936

 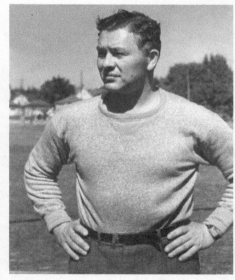

Curly Lambeau (right) awarded what was then the highest contract in Packers history to Don Hutson in 1935. The investment paid off immediately and continued to pay dividends a year later against Boston. WIKIMEDIA COMMONS

To be declared a champion by a committee, by circumstances, or through dumb luck is one thing. To win it on the field where it matters most? There's nothing like it.

The Green Bay Packers understood this only too well.

Make no mistake. This was a team that dominated a league still searching for an identity and consistency, and a place in the hearts and minds of the American sports fan.

But in those formative years, it was a league that looked too much like it couldn't get out of its own way. Franchises would spring up almost overnight, play a season or two in front of sparse crowds, and, again almost overnight, simply disappear, never to be heard from again.

And it was this NFL that the Packers used as their personal chew toy. After winning their first championship in 1929, highlighted by the epic and unexpected win over the New York Giants, they won a second straight title in 1930, this time thanks to a missed extra point in the season-finale 6–6 tie with the Portsmouth Spartans. Had Portsmouth converted its extra point and won the game, the title would have gone to the Giants. Instead, for the second straight year, they had to take a back seat to the Packers.

In 1931 the NFL continued to convulse with change, and the Great Depression, now fully gripping the nation, did not help. Due to financial concerns, the Minneapolis Red Jackets and Newark Tornadoes had to close up shop before the season, and the Frankford Yellow Jackets, a long-standing NFL member, had to fold at midseason.

Even with the addition of the Cleveland Indians that season, the NFL stood at just 10 teams, its lowest membership since it formed 12 years earlier.

But one of the constants remained the Green Bay Packers, who would use a new crop of talented players, including Green Bay native Arnie Herber, to continue their domination.

Thanks to the evolving and devastating combination of quarterback Herber and end Don Hutson, the Packers rang up a 12–2 record, finishing a game ahead of the Portsmouth Spartans and winning their third straight championship.

But while the title the year before came on the strength of a single point, the 1931 title was a little more controversial.

The Packers did not face the Spartans during their regular-season schedule, but Spartans officials claimed a verbal agreement with Lambeau stipulated the two teams would meet each other. Lambeau said there was no such agreement, and the matter went to league President Joe Carr, who ruled in favor of the Packers.

Green Bay, on paper at least, was the first team in the NFL's brief history to win three straight championships, but a sour taste was left in the mouths of many after the 1931 title was essentially decided in a backroom negotiation. It was time to settle the NFL title on the field where it belonged.

Though the league didn't officially start its playoff system until 1933, the first on-field playoff came in 1932 and was not without its own share of controversy—which, of course, featured the Packers peripherally.

In 1932 the NFL was in trouble. Three more teams—the Cleveland Indians, Frankford Yellow Jackets (who had stopped playing at midseason the previous year), and Providence Steam Roller—dropped out of the league and the Boston Braves joined. But that still left just eight teams, which was now the lowest total in league history.

The Packers again were one of the elite teams, posting a 10–3–1 record, which mathematically should have been enough for a fourth straight title.

But the Chicago Bears and Portsmouth Spartans had other ideas—as did the league. The Bears had seven wins, one loss, and six ties while Portsmouth posted six wins, two losses, and four ties.

It was determined that winning percentage, not including the ties, would determine the champion. Both Portsmouth and Chicago, with winning percentages of .875, beat out the Packers and their .769 winning percentage. And since there was a tie, a playoff would be held to decide the champion.

The Bears beat the Spartans 9–0 in a game played indoors in Chicago because it was too cold to play outdoors at Wrigley Field.

The game proved a success despite the circumstances, and in 1933 the NFL was split into two divisions, the Eastern and the Western. That decision was aided by the arrival of three new teams—the Philadelphia Eagles, Pittsburgh Steelers, and Cincinnati Reds—and the departure of the Staten Island Stapletons, giving the league two five-team groups. Simply enough, the winner of each division would meet in a championship game, as it should be.

The Packers, residing in the Western Division along with the Chicago Bears, the Chicago Cardinals, the Portsmouth Spartans (who would become the Detroit Lions the following season), and the Cincinnati Reds, found themselves on the outside looking in when it came to the new playoff format.

The Bears would win the division in 1933 and 1934, and the Lions in 1935, before Green Bay had its resurgence in 1936 thanks in no small part to their acquisition of a receiver who would change not only the Packers but the NFL.

It was still in the days before NFL teams could draft college players, and at that time amateur players could sign with whatever team they wanted.

In 1935 Curly Lambeau had his sights set on a 6-foot-1, 185-pound receiver from the University of Alabama who was fast, smart, and quick. If the term had existed then, Don Hutson would have been known as a "game changer." Instead, they called him the "Alabama Antelope," and the Packers wanted him badly. Then again, so did another team, the Brooklyn Dodgers.

In yet another dispute that had to be uncoiled by league President Joe Carr, it was determined that Hutson go to the Packers, supposedly because Green Bay's contract offer to Hutson had been postmarked earlier.

Whatever the reason, Lambeau was thrilled and proceeded to reward Hutson with the richest contract in team history: $300 per game.

And in another of those stories that every Packers fan knows, Hutson made a thunderous debut, catching an 83-yard touchdown pass from Arnie Herber on his very first reception. That season, Hutson caught 18 passes in nine games but averaged an unheard-of 23 yards per catch. He would only get better.

By the 1936 season, Herber and Hutson had already developed the "chemistry" so crucial between quarterback and receiver. Indeed, of the 77 passes Herber completed that season, 34 went to Hutson and eight of those resulted in touchdowns.

Hutson had made the forward pass a weapon that could no longer be ignored by rival defenses. Led by the Herber-Hutson connection, a balanced running attack paced by Clarke Hinkle, and a defense that allowed fewer than 10 points a game, Green Bay won its first Western Division title with a 10–1–1 record. Herber led the NFL with 1,239 passing yards and Hutson was the top receiver with 536 yards.

That set up the NFL Championship Game with the Boston Redskins, who won the Eastern Division with a nondescript 7–5 record. In fact, the Redskins hadn't exactly set their home fans on fire during the season, and when team owner George Preston Marshall learned the Eastern Division champ would host the game, he made a bewildering decision.

Not willing to play in front of what he expected to be a small, less-than-raucous Boston crowd on a Fenway Park field that was already in terrible shape, he was able to get the game moved to New York's Polo Grounds, a home away from home of sorts for the Packers. After all, the Packers had built quite a following in New York City after their 1929 win over the Giants. A crowd of more than 25,000 showed up, and most were rooting for the Packers.

It really wasn't much of a game.

Herber threw a 48-yard touchdown pass to Hutson in the first quarter to open the scoring, and the Packers were in control. A third-quarter Herber–to–Milt Gantenbein touchdown pass and a fourth-quarter TD run by Bob Monnett, coupled with a defense that allowed just 147 yards and forced three Boston turnovers, would be more than enough for the Packers to claim their fourth NFL championship—but their first that was decided on the field.

When it was over, an emotional Curly Lambeau, for whom offering compliments was about as common as palm trees in Wisconsin, honored his team.

"These Packers are as fine a squad of men as ever represented any city," he said. "They have been marvelous, not only on the football field but in their everyday relations toward their work, their coaches, and the city they represent."

It was a game marked for importance, again, for several reasons. First and foremost, of course, was the opportunity for Green Bay to win its fourth title in an NFL that was still just 17 years old, marking it as one of the league's powerhouses.

Second, it was Green Bay's first chance to win a title on the field, letting the players from both sides make the difference. There were no vagaries of winning percentages and tied games and decisions by people who did not play the game. It was decided fair and square.

For the Packers, a fourth championship—and this one over another team from a major metropolitan area (though the following week Marshall would move his team from Boston to Washington)—provided yet more evidence to national pro football fans that Green Bay might be someplace special.

And two years later the Packers were back in the championship game, despite injuries that hobbled two major stars, Herber and Hutson.

But a new quarterback, Cecil Isbell, rallied the Packers to an 8–3 record, and Hutson, who missed three games due to an injury, still caught 32 passes for a league-best 548 yards and nine touchdowns. But the Packers didn't secure their Western Division title until the Detroit Lions lost their final two games.

That set up Green Bay's second appearance in the NFL Championship Game, this time against its old foe the New York Giants in a game that again would be played at the Polo Grounds. But this time, in front of what was then an NFL-record crowd of 48,120, the Giants hung on to beat the Packers 23–17.

In 1939 the Packers were back again, and while no one, especially a growing legion of Packers fans, knew it at the time, that championship appearance would mark the beginning of a downward trend for the franchise and for the man who created the Packers and their mystique.

The Packers roared through their 1939 schedule, posting a 9–2 record and catching fire toward the end of the regular season when, after a tough midseason loss to the Bears, they won their final four games, outscoring their opponents 70–26.

It set up a championship rematch with the Giants, and a chance for Lambeau to avenge a year-old loss that had festered within him since the moment that game ended.

This time, however, the Packers would get to play host, a major advantage for a game that would be played in mid-December. But even that opportunity would not be without controversy.

Keep in mind that despite having won four titles in the previous 10 seasons, Green Bay remained a franchise struggling to keep its collective head above water financially. That situation had improved some, thanks to a recent 6,000-seat expansion of City Stadium, which now held some 25,000 fans. But it was still the smallest venue in the NFL, and Green Bay was hosting its first NFL Championship Game—so something had to give.

In a decision that left Green Bay fans howling in protest, the team's executive committee made the call to move the Packers-Giants game to Milwaukee's State Fair Park, a stadium that seated more than 32,000 and, yes, was situated in a major city, which Green Bay, at the time, definitely was not.

Green Bay fans were convinced there was some backroom deal made with Milwaukee officials, and some even suggested this was another step toward moving the team permanently from its ancestral home in Green Bay 100 miles south to Milwaukee.

When the decision to move the game was made, four days before it was to be played, team officials tried to explain it was an opportunity to thank the Packers fans down south who had been so loyal for so many years. That only made Green Bay fans angrier.

Nonetheless, on a cold, windy afternoon, the Packers exacted revenge on the Giants. As more than 32,000 fans watched, Green Bay's defense intercepted six passes, quarterbacks Arnie Herber and Cecil Isbell each threw touchdown passes, and the Packers rolled to a dominant 27–0 win.

In the 18 seasons of the NFL's existence, this was the Packers' fifth championship. The New York Giants and Chicago Bears, both residing in major metropolitan markets, each had three, and no other team was even close.

Under Lambeau's leadership, shrewd drafting, and a little luck, the Packers had established themselves as the game's most consistent franchise.

Green Bay was back in contention two years later, tying the Bears for the Western Division's best regular-season record at 10–1. But in a playoff to decide the division winner, Chicago blasted the Packers and went on to win the NFL title.

There was no reason to believe the Packers would not continue their run of success. But as they were about to discover, all good things do indeed come to an end.

CHAPTER THREE

"IT WAS A TEAM EFFORT"

PACKERS 9, CHICAGO BEARS 6

SEPTEMBER 27, 1959

Vince Lombardi celebrates with fans after the first of his 89 career regular-season victories as a head coach in the NFL. AP PHOTO/VERNON BIEVER

MORE OFTEN THAN NOT, NO ONE KNOWS WHAT EVEN CONSTITUTES AN "important" event until well after it happens. Then everyone looks back, analyzes what occurred, and realizes they should have understood its significance from the beginning.

So it was with this game. Historians and pundits and just regular football fans now look at this season-opening win by a first-year coach of a moribund franchise as perhaps the most important in team history.

Of course, those in attendance and/or who read about it would not have said the same thing at the time. But this win signaled that the future of the Green Bay Packers would be changing in major and profound ways.

But first, a look back—all the way back to 1944—when the organization was going through its first truly turbulent time.

In 1944, with a complement of a new generation of talent—including Ted Fritsch at running back and Irv Comp at quarterback—to go with an aging but still dangerous Don Hutson, the Packers posted an 8–2 record and again edged out their perennial rival Chicago Bears for the Western Division title. And for the fourth time in nine seasons, Green Bay was back in the championship with, once again, the Giants as the opposition.

But the star of the Packers' 14–7 win was not any of the players who had made so many headlines over the years. It was Joe Laws, who had spent 11 seasons with the Packers with only middling success. But on the biggest stage of the season, he ran for 74 yards and intercepted three passes from former Packers star Arnie Herber, who was finishing out his career with the Giants.

Comp only completed three passes for the day (and threw three interceptions), but one was a touchdown to Fritsch (who also scored the other touchdown on a one-yard run), and the Packers forced four turnovers and held the Giants to only 199 total yards.

It was another methodical triumph and Green Bay's sixth NFL championship. But storm clouds were gathering even after the Packers' executive committee in early 1945 rewarded Lambeau with a new contract that would run through the 1949 season.

As is often the case, the problems did not hit all at once and with great force. It was, in some respects, death by a thousand cuts—a lot of little things that eventually ended up being something big.

For example, the game's greatest receiver and the Packers' greatest player until that point, Don Hutson, retired after the 1945 season. He had been battling an assortment of injuries for years and admitted he was interested in seeing what else there was in life besides football. Irv Comp's final season was 1949 and Ted Fritsch stepped away in 1950.

But the biggest change was in Lambeau, whose interest in the Packers began to wane—perhaps not surprisingly after he received his contract extension.

Always a tough character to deal with even on his best days, Lambeau became even more of an autocrat, making decisions without consulting the committee, spending more time away from Green Bay, and focusing on living in California, where he had met a new love. He also went through a public, nasty divorce, and his reputation in Wisconsin and around the league began to crack.

He locked horns with the executive committee and the so-called "Hungry Five," a group of local business leaders formed in 1923 who had simply found ways to keep the Packers franchise solvent.

But six championships had Lambeau believing he was bulletproof, and he began making decisions that seemed puzzling at best, ridiculous at worst. This included one of the most infamous moves in team history, when he decided to move the Packers training camp 30 miles north to pastoral and remote Door County and house them in a facility called Rockwood Lodge. The facility, the practice field, and dorms for both married and single players cost the Packers more than $50,000 (which today would be close to $1.5 million). And it was money the perpetually cash-strapped franchise did not have.

The move out of Green Bay infuriated fans, players, and team officials alike, and to make matters worse, the lodge mysteriously burned down in 1950. While the blaze was listed as accidental, there are still stories circulating around Green Bay that a mysterious man, perhaps tied to Lambeau, had something to do with it.

Lambeau also removed franchise cofounder George Calhoun, a staunch ally for years, from any involvement with the franchise. And he didn't even tell Calhoun he was through—Calhoun had to find out in a news report in his own *Green Bay Press-Gazette* newspaper.

In a famous quote that seemed to encapsulate the feelings of many toward the increasingly erratic Lambeau, Calhoun once said, "I just want to live long enough to piss on Lambeau's grave."

These flights of ego and confrontation might have been tolerated if Lambeau had continued to produce winners on the field. But from 1945 through 1947, the Packers finished third in their division and never won more than six games.

And it only got worse. In 1948 the Packers went 3–9, their worst record since joining the NFL, and they broke that mark the following season, managing just two wins in 12 games.

It was that awful 1949 season in which Lambeau, after a season-opening shutout loss to the Bears, relinquished his coaching duties to three of his assistant coaches—Bob Snyder, Tom Stidham, and Charley Brock—so he could concentrate on his other job as general manager.

But it did no good. Nevertheless, after the season the executive committee still voted to extend Lambeau's contract for two more years, though by January 1950 he still hadn't signed it.

Then, on January 30, 1950, citing "dangerous disunity of purpose within the corporation," Lambeau resigned to take over as vice president and head coach of the Chicago Cardinals.

The loss of the founder, the visionary, the coach, and the soul of the Green Bay Packers made a bad situation even worse, and over the next nine seasons and through four head coaches, the Packers would not have a winning season. Indeed, some of the worst football the NFL has ever seen was produced in Green Bay, turning the early NFL gold standard of franchises first into a joke and then, even worse, into irrelevancy.

Which, at last, brings us to September 27, 1959.

Packers fans had come to expect very little from their team. The old-timers remembered better days when the likes of Johnny McNally and Clarke Hinkle and Don Hutson and Arnie Herber would perform magic on the gridiron. But that was long ago and far away, and now the hope was for respectability and perhaps a winning record.

And they had to hope the coach who would bring that about was someone named Vince Lombardi, a New Yorker who came to Wisconsin after most recently serving as offensive coordinator for the New York Giants. He had never been a head coach before and, truly, he wasn't even the first choice of the executive committee to take over a franchise headed nowhere in a hurry.

Indeed, the Packers had spoken with Forest Evashevski, who had enjoyed a successful stint as head coach at the University of Iowa. But those talks broke down, and Lombardi, who had been on the Packers' radar from the start, rose back to the top of the list.

The Giants were reluctant to part with the mercurial but talented Lombardi to the point that team owner Wellington Mara even suggested the Packers discuss their opening with New York's other talented assistant coach, defensive coordinator Tom Landry.

But Lombardi intrigued the Packers with his combination of New York swagger and his deep belief that there was no easy formula for success.

So, after a series of failed head coaches, from Gene Ronzani to Hugh Devore to Ray McLean to Lisle Blackbourn, who between them won 32 games across nine seasons, the Packers settled on Lombardi as not only head coach but with the key duties as general manager as well.

In the background and watching closely was Chicago Bears founder, head coach, and NFL mainstay George Halas, one of the league's original driving forces, who watched Lambeau and the Packers surge to greatness, then fall into mediocrity.

Halas had a particular interest in watching what the Packers were up to as, since 1946, when the Packers' travails really began, the Bears had dominated their rivals to the north, winning 19, losing five, and tying once.

And Halas was furious and anxious when he learned the Packers had hired Lombardi, because he knew deep down everything was going to change. He even told Packers President Dominic Olejniczak, who had fought especially hard to hire Lombardi, "He's going to win you a lot of games."

Halas had hoped he was wrong, but he knew he wasn't.

The stories come fast and furious from this point about Lombardi and his impact on the Packers players, the franchise, the city of Green Bay, and the NFL.

He was a force of nature, blowing ill wind and good, but he changed the culture of a team that had lost a sense of itself.

Quarterback Bart Starr repeated often the first meeting between the team and its new coach when he made a speech that burrowed its way into the brain and psyche of every player.

"Gentlemen, we are always going to relentlessly chase perfection knowing full well we will not catch it because nothing is perfect. In the process, we will catch excellence. I am not remotely interested in being just good."

The speech had a special impact on Starr, a 17th-round draft pick of the Packers in 1956 who in his first three seasons had completed barely 50 percent of his passes while throwing 13 touchdown passes and 25 interceptions. And after the Packers' disastrous 1–10–1 season in 1958 (still the worst in team history), Starr was beginning to consider whether he even belonged in the NFL.

But there was something almost undefinable that told Starr and other players that Lombardi would be different, and giving him the opportunity to implement his plan could well benefit everyone.

That's because the Packers roster was a gold mine of talent, and many of the players already knew it. The team that could only win one game in 1958 already featured the core of what would become the dominant team of the 1960s.

Already in place were offensive linemen Forrest Gregg and Jerry Kramer, halfback Paul Hornung, and fullback Jim Taylor (all of whom now reside in the Pro Football Hall of Fame), as well as wide receiver Max McGee, center Jim Ringo, and linebacker Dan Currie.

As well, the 1958 draft produced a rugged linebacker from the University of Illinois, Ray Nitschke, and the 1959 draft would bring in a fast, sure-handed flanker from the University of Colorado, a wide receiver named Boyd Dowler.

So the pieces were in place for the Packers to not only get better but to get better quickly—if the right coach could be found to mix those ingredients properly. The players certainly knew this and, more important, so did Lombardi.

Another player who was eager to buy into what Lombardi was selling was Paul Hornung, who, like Starr, had languished for two seasons with a coaching staff that didn't know how to properly utilize his skills.

Hornung had been a celebrated college player, the Heisman Trophy winner in 1956 for a mediocre Notre Dame team in which he led the Irish in rushing, passing, scoring, kickoff and punt returns, kicking, and punting. He was also their best player on defense from his safety spot.

He had been selected by the Packers in the supplemental draft and was reluctant to go to a bad team in an NFL backwater, but he had always wanted to be a pro football player and this was his opportunity.

But Hornung and coach Lisle Blackbourn clashed from the start in 1957. Blackbourn wasn't sure exactly what to do with Hornung. Was he a quarterback? A halfback? A fullback? Should he play defense?

During that 3–9 season, Hornung never got comfortable anywhere and ended up rushing only 60 times for 319 yards and catching just six passes. Blackbourn was fired after that season and Ray McLean took over, but nothing really changed for Hornung.

He rushed for another 300 yards, caught a few passes, and watched the train wreck that was the 1958 season.

"It was worse than anything I could have imagined," he said in *The Paul Hornung Scrapbook*. "I didn't want to keep going through this."

In fact, Hornung, who had already been dubbed "The Golden Boy" by a local sportswriter while in college, was already wondering if there was another career for him besides the interminable agony of losing with the Packers.

He was smart, attractive, and well-spoken and there were some, including himself, who thought he might have a career in acting, an industry that paid well, would utilize his talents, and didn't require him to have his brains beaten out every Sunday.

But he wanted to give his pro career, and Lombardi, a chance. He was especially intrigued when he received a letter from the new coach, weeks before the start of 1959 training camp.

The letter, typed neatly and formally enough to make it clear the new guy meant business, told Hornung to come to camp in shape and ready to work because, unlike the previous two seasons, Lombardi knew exactly where Hornung should play.

In part the letter said: "I suggest you report to training camp at a maximum of 207 pounds. You will be heavy enough at that weight and left halfback in my system must have speed in order to capitalize on the running pass option play."

With that, the question was answered for Hornung. That letter told him he'd be a running back—the featured running back, he presumed—in an offense that would predominantly feature running the ball. That's all he wanted. And now Hornung was all in, as were most of the other Packers who had suffered through the previous tortuous season.

Keep in mind that the team that went 1–10–1 in 1958 under McLean featured players who would one day become legendary—though, obviously, no one knew it at the time.

Still, that team had players such as offensive linemen Forrest Gregg, Jerry Kramer, and Jim Ringo; Starr at quarterback; Jim Taylor and Hornung in the backfield; and Ray Nitschke at linebacker. All would wind up in the Pro Football Hall of Fame. But there were other quality players like defensive back Jesse Whittenton and Bobby Dillon; linebacker Bill Forester; wide receivers Max McGee and Billy Howton; and defensive tackle Dave Hanner.

It would take someone like Lombardi to find that talent and bring it to the surface. And he knew that when that happened, he would have a team for the ages. It began by changing the culture and instilling a long-absent feeling of winning. And the most decisive way to do that was to change the roster.

For example, Howton, who had caught 303 passes and averaged more than 18 yards a catch the previous seven seasons in Green Bay, was traded to the Cleveland Browns for running back Lew Carpenter and defensive end Bill Quinlan. Lombardi also traded with the Chicago Cardinals for the services of quarterback Lamar McHan because, as he admitted at the time, he just wasn't sure he could win with Bart Starr.

He also brought in future Hall of Fame defensive back Emlen Tunnell from the New York Giants; guard Fuzzy Thurston from the Baltimore Colts; and defensive tackle Henry Jordan from the Browns.

Indeed, by the time training camp began that season, some 16 veteran players from the previous season were no longer on the roster. But that was only part of it. The key would be how this new roster would meld together as a team.

It had to start somewhere. And that somewhere was the corner of Oneida Street and Highland Avenue, where, two years earlier, the franchise had christened its new stadium.

It was a time of hope and enthusiasm then as the residents of Green Bay—convinced a new, larger stadium was needed to keep their beloved (if flawed) team in town—supported a bond referendum in 1956 to build a $900,000 playpen that would seat some 32,000 fans. It was a major upgrade for the old, deteriorating City Stadium, but the new place would also be called City Stadium, and, after a promising 6–6 record in 1955, there was hope the new stadium would lead to better times.

It did not.

The 1956 Packers managed only a 4–8 record and were just 3–9 in 1957 before the bottom completely fell out in 1958.

So now it was time to start—again—and a full house of 32,150 showed up on September 27, 1959, to watch a new team with a new coach but with an unshakable feeling that it would be the same old results.

And, to be honest, it was not exactly a game for the ages. The Chicago Bears were coming off a solid season and, like the Packers, would emphasize the running game. But it was an ugly, mistake-filled contest that neither team seemed intent on controlling.

McHan, who in training camp had beaten out Starr as the starting quarterback, overthrew open receivers, tossed a bad interception, and completed just 3 of 12 passes for 81 yards, though one went for 67 yards to Max McGee.

But it was not an epic struggle. Paul Hornung missed two short field goal attempts and a third never got off the ground due to a bad snap.

The Bears could generate nothing on offense, committing two turnovers of their own while managing just two field goals.

Still, it appeared that would be enough for the Bears, who led Green Bay 6–0 midway through the fourth quarter. But with seven minutes remaining in the game, Chicago's Richie Petitbon fumbled on a punt return deep in Green Bay territory and Jim Ringo recovered.

In what proved to be a precursor for a golden future, fullback Jim Taylor (who ran for 98 yards on 22 carries for the game) swept left and into the end zone from the Bears' five on a play that would come to be known as the "Packers Sweep." The play would be run a thousand times in stadiums around the league over the next decade.

Hornung's extra point gave Green Bay the lead, and just a few minutes later Dave Hanner would engulf Bears quarterback Ed Brown in his own end zone for a safety that would provide the winning margin.

When it was over, the Packers did something fans had not seen in a long time: grown men jumped up and down in giddy excitement and carried their new coach off the field. An emotional Jim Ringo presented Lombardi with the game ball. It was exhilaration in its purest form.

"You have no idea how important that game was to us," guard Jerry Kramer said. "It changed everything."

For his part, Lombardi stewed about all the mistakes and missed opportunities, though he was pleased that the defense had held the Bears to just 164 total yards.

"It was a team effort," Lombardi said simply.

But he meant that in more ways than most knew. That's because Lombardi knew that football was the epitome of a team sport and every player had to work together toward a common goal to be successful. Losing as a team built character, but winning as a team built confidence, and he knew this was a start, especially defeating a longtime rival like the Bears.

The excitement continued to build in the following weeks in Green Bay as the Packers proceeded to beat the Detroit Lions and then rallied for a fourth-quarter touchdown to edge the San Francisco 49ers. Under the new coach the Packers were 3–0 for the first time since 1944, which was also the last year the Packers claimed an NFL title.

But greatness is not built overnight or even in one season.

A week after beating the 49ers, the Packers played before a wild throng at Milwaukee County Stadium and were clobbered, 45–6, by the Los Angeles Rams. Reality had introduced itself—it came in, sat down, and made itself comfortable. The offense committed four turnovers and gained just 262 total yards while the defense surrendered nearly 500 yards of offense to the Rams.

Worse, the Packers allowed 24 fourth-quarter points and, in places he didn't want to acknowledge, Lombardi began to think his new team had quit on him. It was not a pleasant thought.

But it was the adversity Lombardi knew would eventually arise even as he constantly drummed into his team, "I have never been part of a losing team and I don't intend to start now." Now he'd see how his new team would handle it. He got the answer soon enough.

Four more losses in a row would follow—first to the Baltimore Colts, then to the New York Giants, followed by a thumping at the hands of the Chicago Bears, and then again to the Colts.

Five straight losses wasn't necessarily a surprise to long-suffering Packers fans, since, after all, losing streaks had become commonplace for the franchise.

But not for Lombardi. Indeed, the losing streak he suffered through his first season in Green Bay would be the longest the franchise would experience through his 10 years as head coach. In fact, the Packers would not lose five consecutive games again until 1977.

But as difficult as the streak was, it was the kind of learning experience that proved invaluable for both the coach and his players.

During that streak, the worst of the Packers appeared and took shape. On offense, they averaged just 296 yards and 19 points per game and committed a staggering 19 turnovers, while the defense allowed 32 points and 354 yards per game.

But in this slow, agonizing march toward respectability, something was taking root and it showed in Green Bay's fifth straight loss, a 28–24 defeat at the hands of the Colts.

In that game Lombardi decided—partially out of desperation and partially out of curiosity—that Bart Starr would get the start in place of the injured McHan and an unknown Joe Fields.

Starr threw three interceptions but also passed for 242 yards and a touchdown. More importantly, the running game that Lombardi knew would be the ticket to his new team's success began to click. Fullback Jim Taylor ran for 79 yards and two touchdowns and Paul Hornung ran for another 77 yards.

The following week Green Bay ended its skid by blanking the Washington Redskins, 21–0. Starr threw two more touchdown passes, and Taylor and Hornung combined to rush for another 159 yards.

From there the Packers would win their final three games of the season, beating the Detroit Lions, gaining revenge over the Rams, who had embarrassed them earlier in the season, and then berating the San Francisco 49ers.

By the end of the season, Taylor and Hornung were established backs, the defense had found its bearings, and Starr had taken command as the starting quarterback.

It was the beginning of a dynasty. The Packers finished that season 7–5, their first winning campaign since 1947, and Lombardi was a unanimous pick as NFL Coach of the Year. Over the next nine seasons, Green Bay would go to six NFL championship games, winning five of them, and become the gold standard of what a great NFL team could be.

Perhaps the five-game losing streak brought everything into focus, but the true key that season was the opener against the Bears when, against all odds and expectations, they won a game they had no business winning.

And everything flowed from there.

Perhaps Packers All-Pro guard Fuzzy Thurston said it best years later when he told the *New York Times*, "We realized in his first season that we were going to be a very good team. Lombardi wasn't going to stand for anything less."

CHAPTER FOUR

"IT WAS A HELL OF A FOOTBALL GAME"

PACKERS 16, NEW YORK GIANTS 7

DECEMBER 30, 1962

Jerry Kramer kicks a field goal during the 1962 NFL Championship Game against the Giants.
AP PHOTO/VERNON BIEVER

It had been so long—too long—for many long-suffering Green Bay Packers fans. Their beloved heroes had been through hell and back in the previous 20 years or so. From the heights of seemingly perennial NFL championships in the 1930s and 1940s, the Packers had fallen into a quagmire of bad players, bad decisions, and bad football.

Now a new decade had dawned and the Pack, to borrow a phrase, seemed to be back. But not all the way. Not yet.

Under the fiery and uncompromising leadership of head coach Vince Lombardi, Green Bay had enjoyed a renaissance. A 7–5 record in his first season in 1959 was followed by an unexpected 8–4 mark in 1960 and a trip to the NFL championship against the Philadelphia Eagles—their first appearance in the title game since 1944. But the job was not completed as the Packers, despite outplaying the host Eagles, fell 17–13.

Remember Willie Davis's favorite story? It was in the locker room after that loss that Lombardi addressed his disappointed team and said simply that as long as he was head coach of the Packers, they would never lose another championship game.

Which brings us to a bend in the road. In the list of important games in Packers history, there are, of course, degrees and, yes, a certain context with which they must be viewed.

This 1962 game is indeed one of the most important in franchise history, but frankly, the matchup against the New York Giants cannot be analyzed without first looking at the 1961 NFL Championship—also against the Giants.

"That '61 championship really got people's attention," said Packers team historian Cliff Christl.

And by "people" he meant the national sports media, which was the currency of the realm at the time. To make a mark on the national media scale, and specifically with East Coast media (read that as New York), something truly special had to be occurring. Once viewed in that prism, the sky was the limit.

So, before talking about the overall importance of the 1962 championship, let's take a brief detour to 1961 and label that a "game of great significance bordering on the truly important."

It was December 31, 1961. The renaissance of the Green Bay Packers under Lombardi was continuing unabated. A good team was getting better thanks to key trades and decent drafting. Indeed, the first round of the 1961 draft netted the Packers a starting defensive back and eventual Pro Football Hall of Famer in Herb Adderley; a solid, dependable defensive tackle in Ron Kostelnik in the second round; and an eventual starting running back deep in the 13th round in Elijah Pitts.

The pieces were connecting nicely, and with the memory of the agonizing loss the year before in Philadelphia, the Packers not only had the talent but a common, burning goal.

The Packers shook off an opening-day loss to the Detroit Lions and won their next six on the way to an 11–3 regular-season record—their highest win total since they won 12 games back in 1931.

That set up the NFL Championship Game with the Eastern Division champion New York Giants, who had posted a solid 10–4–1 mark behind the league's top quarterback, Y. A. Tittle, and a strong defense.

But having the better overall record, the Packers would host the championship game, the first ever in Green Bay (the Packers had won the 1939 title game played in Milwaukee) and the excitement was palpable.

"Everyone in Green Bay was excited," Christl recalled. "People weren't talking about anything else."

Three years earlier, this same franchise had managed just one win.

But that was then, this was now, and the Packers knew that to avoid the same fate as they had the year before, they needed a better overall performance, fewer mistakes, and a full commitment to getting the job done.

This season the Packers were also seeing the full potential of the running attack Lombardi had envisioned when he first came to the team. Fullback Jim Taylor bulled his way to 1,305 yards on the ground and 15 touchdowns, while Paul Hornung ran for another 598 yards and eight TDs and led the league in scoring thanks to his kicking duties.

The defense was opportunistic and nasty, intercepting 29 passes and recovering 25 fumbles, and Lombardi had learned some lessons himself from the previous year.

In the 1960 title game, whether it was due to stubbornness or hubris or simple inexperience, he passed up opportunities to kick field goals against the Eagles at crucial junctures of the game. Those opportunities backfired and Lombardi blamed himself for that loss. And Lombardi never forgot the decisions he made, or more important, the decisions he did not make.

But even with all that going for them, as well as home-field advantage, the Packers were three-point underdogs to the Giants. That actually seemed appropriate when it became a likelihood the Packers would have to play the game without Hornung, who was scheduled the weekend of the game to fulfill his military requirement with the Army at Fort Riley, Kansas.

Hornung recalled this years later in his book, *The Paul Hornung Scrapbook*.

"When I told Lombardi I wasn't sure I could get away, I figured it was all over. But Lombardi had met President [John] Kennedy and they really hit it off. They really admired each other. Kennedy actually gave Vince his private phone number and told him to call if he ever needed anything."

As it turned out, Lombardi needed something.

No one really knows the specifics of what happened next, not even Hornung, but two days before the game, Hornung was on a plane from Kansas back to Green Bay.

"Lombardi never talked about it," Hornung recalled years later. "He didn't have to."

It was a day Lombardi referred to as "our kind of day," six-degree windchill and a frozen field on which the Giants could never gain their footing despite their coaches' brainstorm that they wear sneakers instead of cleats.

Paul Hornung, fresh from his military reprieve, scored one touchdown, kicked three field goals, added four extra points, and scored what was then an NFL playoff record 19 points (a record that stood for

56 years) in Green Bay's 37–0 demolition of the Giants. But that wasn't enough for Hornung.

"I was mad at Vince," Hornung related to the *Milwaukee Journal Sentinel* years later. "We could have scored 70 against them but he pulled the starters out early. He liked the Maras [the family who owned the Giants and who had hired Lombardi years earlier as offensive coordinator] and didn't want to rub it in. We had a tremendous team and we played a tremendous game."

In front of a national TV audience, the Packers dominated Lombardi's old team, holding them to 130 total yards, intercepting Tittle four times, and giving the Packers their first world title since 1944. And as they had done in their first win for their new coach two years earlier, Packers players carried Lombardi off the field in triumph as the home crowd at City Stadium roared its approval.

"The fans really got into it," Davis recalled in the book *Game of My Life*. "I would say it was a love affair that day. They were having a ball and it was the greatest memory I had in football."

After years of frustration, anger, and uncertainty about the very future of the franchise, the Packers were champions again.

It also got the attention of the national media, who were curious and intrigued about what was transpiring in this little NFL outpost that had been so irrelevant for so long.

"That 1961 championship game really got attention," Christl said.

That decisive victory over the Giants resonated through the NFL, much like the Packers win over this same franchise had done in 1939. And by 1962 the Packers had taken their place as the NFL's newest darling, and Lombardi was heralded as something very close to a miracle worker.

"In 1962 *Time* magazine came to Green Bay and Lombardi ended up on the cover," Christl said.

Indeed, the December 21, 1962, issue carried the headline "The Sport of the '60s," and on the cover was Lombardi.

"It was 1962 when pro football captured national attention again and the Packers were leading it," Christl said. "It was just a remarkable turnaround. I cannot imagine an NFL coach on the cover of *Time* magazine before and it was a huge deal. You had writers coming from all the national publications to write about the Packers and he was a favorite of [renowned national sports columnists] Red Smith and Jim Murray. He was already a larger than life personality."

That was an important game in the history of the Green Bay Packers franchise. But the following season, and the championship to follow, was even more important for several reasons.

By 1962 there was no longer any doubt: Lombardi had built a powerhouse. Fans around the country who were becoming more and more enamored of the sport were seeing it, but more to the point, the Packers players knew it, too. They saw that this may well be a team for the ages.

The Packers had again established themselves as the team to beat in the NFL and the evidence was there for all to see. Fans had returned. The pride was back. The national media was taking notice. Vince Lombardi was in full and complete control. And the players knew what they had and where they could potentially be headed.

"I think if you go back, you'd see that most of the players would tell you the '62 team was their best," Christl said.

Few would argue. This was, after all, a roster loaded from top to bottom and that included 10 First-Team All-Pros—five on offense and five on defense.

On offense they included fullback Jim Taylor, center Jim Ringo, tight end Ron Kramer, right guard Jerry Kramer, and right tackle Forrest Gregg. Left off were quarterback Bart Starr, halfback Paul Hornung, left guard Fuzzy Thurston, and wide receiver Boyd Dowler.

On defense? It included defensive end Willie Davis, tackle Henry Jordan, linebackers Bill Forester and Dan Currie, and cornerback Herb Adderley. Left off were linebacker Ray Nitschke and safety Willie Wood, who only intercepted nine passes that season.

All told, 11 players (and the head coach) on that 1962 Packers roster would find a place in the Pro Football Hall of Fame.

So, the defending NFL champs came in loaded and ready to win a second straight title.

Interestingly enough, in the Western Division their goal would be blocked by an unexpected source. Usually, it was the Chicago Bears,

Green Bay's ancient rival, who offered the Packers their biggest challenge. But since 1960 the Detroit Lions had built a fearsome defense and a strong offense and would prove to be a formidable challenge indeed, especially that season.

"I think that while a lot of the Packers then thought this was the best Green Bay team, I think a majority of them would also say the '62 Lions were the best they ever faced," Christl said. "The Lions defense of the '60s was as good as any in the league."

And in 1962 it may have been the best in the league. It featured a ferocious front four that included All-Pros Roger Brown and Alex Karras; a secondary that included safety Yale Lary and cornerbacks Dick "Night Train" Lane and Dick LeBeau, who between them had 16 interceptions that season; and middle linebacker Joe Schmidt, who at age 30 was still among the league's best.

That season the Packers and Lions waged two terrific battles. The first was played October 7 on a rainy, muddy field in Green Bay.

"It was a classic defensive game," Christl recalls. "I still consider it the best game I've ever seen at Lambeau Field [still City Stadium at the time until being renamed in 1965]. I was 15. Ron Wolf [the future Packers general manager] was at that game. He drove up from Chicago to watch it. It was a big game going in and the expectation was that it would settle the conference race if not the championship. It lived up to its billing."

Both teams headed into the game unbeaten and neither had really been challenged. The Lions had outscored their opponents 119–51 while the Packers had prevailed 106–7.

And for most of the game, it appeared the Lions defense would get the better of the Packers' fiery offense. Green Bay had turned the ball over four times, twice on fumbles and twice on option passes by Tom Moore and Paul Hornung.

With six minutes remaining in the game, the Lions took control of the ball on their 22-yard line after a missed Hornung field goal. Quarterback Milt Plum completed two crucial third-down passes to keep possession and the Lions seemed poised to post the upset and what most certainly would have been a statement victory.

But with 1:53 remaining and facing yet another third down near midfield, Plum threw a pass to Terry Barr, who fell down before it got there. Packers cornerback Herb Adderley stepped in and intercepted the pass at the Green Bay 42 and returned it 40 yards to the Detroit 18.

With 33 seconds remaining, Hornung hit a 21-yard field goal to give Green Bay the victory.

It was Green Bay's first test of the season and they had passed—barely. But over the next six weeks, the challenges would be few and far between until the traditional Thanksgiving Day game between the Packers and the host Lions.

The rematch would be decidedly different from the first meeting. Inspired and seeking revenge, the Lions jumped all over the unprepared Packers to the delight of a packed house at Tiger Stadium.

Banged up and fairly disinterested with just four days to prepare for the annual affair, the Packers committed five turnovers, and quarterback Bart Starr was sacked an incredible nine times, as the Lions rolled out to a 26–0 lead after three quarters.

A feeble fourth-quarter Packers rally fell short and Green Bay's hopes for an undefeated season were dashed with the 26–14 defeat.

Interestingly enough, that loss was just another step in the decision to end the Lions-Packers Thanksgiving Day game, which the two teams had played every year since 1951. Lombardi hated it because he believed playing on a Thursday after a Sunday game simply did not leave enough time to recover and prepare to play.

So after the 1963 game between the two teams, which ended in a 13–13 tie, the NFL ended the requirement that Green Bay play on Thanksgiving, opening it up for other league teams to take part. And it wasn't until 1984 that the Packers and Lions again played each other on that holiday.

But that loss in 1962 was the only bump in the road for these Packers. Three more victories would follow, and the Packers would roll into the playoffs with a glittering 13–1 record and as kings of the Western Division for the third straight season.

And again, the roadblock to a second straight league title were the New York Giants. The Packers had faced the Giants the year before in Green Bay for the championship and simply embarrassed the visitors, 37–0.

In 1962 the Giants, who roared through the Eastern Conference with a 12–2 record, had been enveloped with simple, primal revenge. They wanted to face the Packers again and do to them what had been done to them a year earlier.

That opportunity came on December 30, 1962, at Yankee Stadium in the same kind of weather Lombardi always called Packers weather: 25 degrees, 8-degree windchill, 25-mile-an-hour winds that blew over the wooden benches on the sidelines, and a chance for snow.

You know, Packers weather.

A second straight championship was obviously important to the Packers, but for Lombardi, New York City born and raised, it was also a chance to come home and prove what he had believed all along: that he was a great pro football head coach.

New York still flowed through Lombardi. He had gone to high school in Brooklyn and graduated from Fordham University in the Bronx. He had been a high school teacher as well as a football and basketball coach in nearby Englewood, New Jersey, and after several stops along the way, from 1954 to 1958 he was offensive coordinator for the Giants. And deep down, it was always his hope and dream to return to the city he loved to be the head coach of the team he knew so well.

Indeed, even when he accepted the head coach/general manager job with the Packers in 1959, there was a belief among many— Lombardi and Giants management included—that when the Giants head coaching job opened, he would be in line for it.

That's exactly what happened prior to the 1961 season, fresh off Green Bay's stunning appearance in the NFL Championship Game against Philadelphia.

But the verbal deal that Giants owner Wellington Mara (and close friend of Lombardi) believed was in place with Packers president Dominic Olejniczak was apparently news to the Packers brass. Olejniczak said he knew of no agreement regarding Lombardi and the Giants moved on, hiring Allie Sherman instead.

So, a return trip to New York to face the Giants, again, was huge for Lombardi. It was important for him and his team to prove that the previous season was no fluke and that the Packers were a franchise built for the long haul.

As in 1961, there were questions as to whether star halfback and kicker Paul Hornung would be available to play. The previous year, it was a bureaucratic battle with the United States Army that was apparently resolved by a phone call from President Kennedy. This season, it was Hornung's health.

He had been bothered much of the season with nagging injuries, and by the time of the title game, his knee was giving him fits to the point where it was believed he wouldn't be able to play at all against the Giants.

But he did, manning his usual spot at halfback along with Jim Taylor at fullback. He did not handle his usual field goal duties, though; they were taken by right guard Jerry Kramer, who had kicked a fair share in college.

It would prove to be a brutal slugfest of a game in which the weather played a factor but which ultimately relied on the right leg of an offensive lineman turned kicker.

"I was never hit as hard as I was in that game," Taylor said in the book *Game of My Life*. "It was brutal, just brutal."

He suffered a gash to his right arm that required eight stitches to close, and he was bleeding from the mouth from a lacerated tongue. But he also pounded out 85 yards on 31 carries and scored Green Bay's only touchdown. Just days after the game, he spent time in the hospital after contracting hepatitis.

Hornung, who wasn't even supposed to play, rushed for 35 yards and completed a crucial 21-yard pass to Boyd Dowler that set up the Packers' only touchdown.

In the end, though, it was the Packers defense, which forced three Giants turnovers, and Kramer who made the difference.

Kramer, despite the swirling winds inside Yankee Stadium, hit three of five field goal attempts—from 26, 29, and 30 yards—the last coming with a little more than two minutes to play to seal the victory.

In the book *Game of My Life*, Kramer recalled the surreal experience of kicking field goals in a championship game.

"I knew if I made that field goal, we would likely win the game," he said of his final kick. "I remember [fellow guard] Fuzzy Thurston came up to me before the kick and said, 'This is the ballgame, Jerry. Keep your head down, buddy.' It was a wonderful moment."

The Packers had taken the best the Giants had to offer and prevailed, and Green Bay had its eighth NFL championship and finished with 14 victories, a franchise record until 2011 when the Packers won 15 games.

"We had two championships in a row and we didn't see any reason why we couldn't make it three in a row," Hornung said in his book *The Paul Hornung Scrapbook*. "We were at the peak of our game and we saw no end in sight."

But a phone call that off-season from NFL commissioner Pete Rozelle to Hornung changed everything.

There was an end in sight, although no one really knew it at the time.

CHAPTER FIVE

"EVERYONE KNEW EXACTLY WHAT WAS AT STAKE"

PACKERS 21, DALLAS COWBOYS 17

DECEMBER 31, 1967

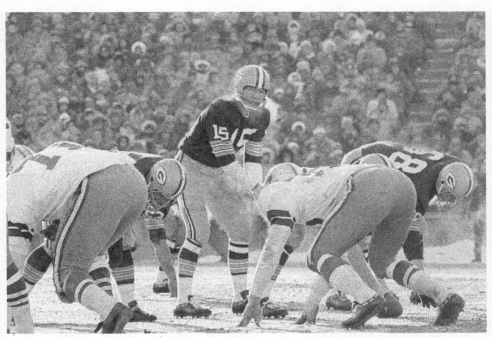

Bart Starr calls signals in the bitter cold of Lambeau Field. AP PHOTO/FILE

THERE IS LITTLE THAT HAS NOT BEEN SAID, WRITTEN, OR ARGUED about what many believe is not only the most important game in Green Bay Packers history but perhaps the most important game in NFL history.

It is a game, even more than five decades later, that still conjures up all the images that made pro football so mesmerizing for so many, and a game that still resonates with players today, often for reasons they cannot understand.

This game, known forever and always as the "Ice Bowl," incorporated so many different elements of the human condition that it is often forgotten that, as Packers defensive end Willie Davis often said, "It really wasn't a very good game."

Stylistically, it certainly was not. The 30-below windchill froze the field into the consistency of cement. Players could barely function, much less excel. There was a period of time when the Packers could manage nothing on offense for two and a half quarters and the Cowboys, when they got over the shock of having to play in these inhuman conditions, could not make a defensive stop on the biggest play in Packers history.

The Ice Bowl remains memorable, historic, vital, important, and a testament to a team's ability to overcome the elements, both physical and mental, to finish a job that needed to be completed.

But to get to that game requires stepping back in time because nothing, even in the NFL, happens in a vacuum.

The setting for the frozen dramatics on the last day of 1967 were set in motion in January 1964. That's when Packers star running back Paul Hornung was summoned to a phone call while dining with teammates Jim Taylor and Bart Starr and their wives in Los Angeles. They were celebrating their rugged NFL title victory over the New York Giants a few weeks earlier, a win that had given the Packers two straight championships with visions of a third for the next season.

But the phone call was from NFL commissioner Pete Rozelle and he was asking Hornung to return to New York as soon as possible. They needed to have a conversation. Hornung had a pretty good idea what that conversation would be about and he knew what it could mean to himself, to the Packers, to his head coach, and to the NFL.

The resulting conversation was a thunderbolt. Rozelle asked Hornung if he had gambled on NFL games and, stunned by the question, he lied and said no.

But Rozelle already had evidence of Hornung's activities and, knowing the problems pro sports were having with gamblers that often included talk of the Mafia, Rozelle was determined to make sure the NFL would not be caught in that web.

Eventually Hornung admitted that, in fact, he had placed a bet with a friend of his in Las Vegas, but he strenuously denied he had any dealing with the Mafia in terms of gambling.

But the damage had been done. Rozelle lowered the boom on Hornung as well as on Detroit Lions All-Pro defensive tackle Alex Karras. Rozelle said both players would be suspended "indefinitely," a term that stunned Hornung because there was no end date in sight. Rozelle said he would reevaluate the situation after the 1963 season.

Hornung's suspension was devastating not only for his career but for the Packers and for the man who had begun to look at Hornung like another son, coach Vince Lombardi.

Without Hornung, the Packers would be without a triple threat on offense. He had finally found his place in Green Bay's offense and he was thriving. Hornung was a threat to run, to pass, to catch the ball out of the backfield. And yes, he was still Green Bay's best placekicker.

But the Packers would have to figure things out in 1963 without him.

On the surface it appears they did. The Packers had another great season, rolling to an 11–2–1 record, which in most seasons would have been good enough to win a fourth straight division title. But not this year.

Both of Green Bay's losses came at the hands of the Chicago Bears. The Packers managed to score just 10 points in those two losses, and the Bears, with a defense that featured five first-team All-Pros, won the division with an 11–1–2 mark. The Packers didn't go quietly, winning their season finale in San Francisco and following reports of the

Bears-Lions game on their plane ride back. But the Bears prevailed and Green Bay was on the outside looking in.

Would the addition of Hornung and his multipronged skills have made a difference? Who knows? But the questions were asked anyway.

Hornung was reinstated for the 1964 season, but it was a year where nothing really seemed to mesh for the Packers. Part of it was injuries—especially to the offensive line that saw star guard Jerry Kramer miss the entire season due to an intestinal issue and tackle Fuzzy Thurston miss five games.

The offensive line was also in upheaval after the trade in May of 1964 of another All-Pro, center Jim Ringo, to the Philadelphia Eagles for linebacker Lee Roy Caffey and a first-round draft pick (which would end up being running back/kicker Donny Anderson).

It also led to one of the great stories in Packers annals that, on the surface, sounded plausible but was very likely just another fable about Vince Lombardi and the autocratic power he had to enforce his will. It's another tale with which most Packers fans of any age are familiar.

The story went that after the 1963 season, in which Ringo again flourished at center and earned All-Pro recognition, Ringo went to Lombardi seeking a new contract and a raise. In those days precious few players had agents and those who did were looked on as just a step up from pond scum in the eyes of many NFL general managers. Lombardi was no different.

But Ringo was his own man. He believed his performance for the Packers over his 11 seasons with the team spoke for itself. He had suffered through some of the worst teams the Packers could ever field and came out the other side as a seven-time All-Pro. And now he wanted a new deal.

Again, the tale is better than the truth. It goes that Ringo went to Lombardi, who was also the team's general manager, and asked for the raise. Lombardi supposedly excused himself from his office, stepped into another room, returned five minutes later, and said to Ringo, "Congratulations, Jim. I just traded you to the Philadelphia Eagles."

It's a great story that grew to legendary proportions over the years as a way to show no one dictated anything to Lombardi.

49

In truth, as it came out over the years, Ringo was a native of the Philadelphia area and was hoping to close out his career with the Eagles and so asked for the trade.

And while he got what he was looking for, the Packers would find themselves depleted on the line and had to move Bob Skoronski, normally a tackle, to center.

It was just one of many little things in 1964 that simply didn't work for whatever reason. Jim Taylor continued to run like a madman, rushing for 1,169 yards (it would be his last of five straight 1,000-yard seasons) and 12 scores, and quarterback Bart Starr had a solid season with 2,144 passing yards, 15 TD passes, and just four interceptions.

And it seemed like the season would go well after the Packers dominated the defending NFL champion Chicago Bears 23–12 in the season opener at City Stadium. But Green Bay would lose three of its next five games, including two by a total of four points to the eventual Western Conference Champion Baltimore Colts, and the season never truly got back on track.

Green Bay would finish with an 8–5–1 mark, the second-worst in Lombardi's nine seasons with the Packers, and end up tied for second in the division with the Minnesota Vikings.

It was, in just about every sense of the word, a wake-up call for the proud franchise.

But 1965 proved to be a surreal, exhilarating, and controversial season on many fronts—not just for the Packers but for the NFL in general.

This was the season the upstart rival American Football League, now in its sixth season, was starting to make inroads with football fans and college talent.

The AFL signed a stunning and lucrative TV deal with NBC starting in 1965 that gave further credence and legitimacy to the league. It also lured one of college football's top young players, University of Alabama quarterback Joe Namath, as he signed with the New York Jets of the AFL instead of the NFL's St. Louis Cardinals, which had also drafted him.

As well, the new league sought to encroach on the Packers' neighborhood, putting out feelers to place a team in Milwaukee, a mere

90 miles from Green Bay. But Lombardi stepped in to claim territorial rights and the plan dissolved.

Meanwhile the Packers, after missing the playoffs for two straight years, returned with a new resolve. They knew they were still among the NFL's top teams but, for reasons that ranged from injury to inconsistency to bad luck, they had not capitalized on opportunities. And the window for NFL teams to succeed does not stay open forever.

The Packers roared into the 1965 season with a vengeance, again relying on a stifling defense that in the end allowed an average of just 16 points a game and forcing a staggering 50 turnovers in 14 games.

Green Bay wasted no time setting its agenda, posting a 6–0 record and finishing the regular season 10–3–1. Unfortunately for the Packers, the defending conference champion Colts also went 10–3–1, and in the days before tiebreakers to establish conference champs, the Colts and Packers had to meet for a third time that season to decide the conference winner.

It would be a game to remember and played in a venue now known as Lambeau Field, which had been rededicated that previous August for the former Packers founder/player/coach who had died two months earlier. And even that was not without its contentiousness.

The renaming of the former "New" City Stadium annoyed Lombardi because of his dislike of Lambeau, whom he believed had not been a great role model for the franchises or the NFL. After all, Lambeau was well known for his extramarital affairs, his battles with the Packers board of directors, a scandalous divorce, and the unceremonious way he left the franchise, departing Green Bay to coach the hapless Chicago Cardinals.

But Lambeau was still Lambeau, and his impact on the team, on the city, and on the state encompassed everything. He had brought little Green Bay, Wisconsin, into the professional sports spotlight, and more to the point, he had made the Packers a household name across the country.

And while even Lombardi could acknowledge that, his hope was that, in time, the stadium would be named after him. Instead, he had to settle, three years later, for the honor of having the road that ran past the new Lambeau Field known as Highland Avenue to bear his name. It would always and forever be known as Lombardi Avenue.

"Usually you name things after people who are already dead," Lombardi said at that ceremony in 1968. "I assure you, I'm not dead yet."

The playoff game to decide who would face the Cleveland Browns for the 1965 NFL Championship Game was played the day after Christmas in typical Green Bay weather—22 degrees, a slight wind, and a windchill of 12. Not bad, really.

But the Colts, who had already lost to the Packers twice in the regular season, came into the game physically shattered. Quarterback John Unitas was already lost due to a knee injury suffered several weeks earlier. And in the next-to-last regular-season game, a loss to the Packers, backup quarterback Gary Cuozzo was lost to a separated shoulder.

In the season finale for the Colts, a gritty 20–17 win over the Los Angeles Rams that secured a division tie with Green Bay, Baltimore used journeyman Ed Brown and starting halfback Tom Matte at quarterback and a stifling defense to somehow hang on.

But in the third meeting against Green Bay, it all fell to Matte to run the offense when it became clear Cuozzo would not be healthy enough to play.

There was nothing pretty about this game. Green Bay played poorly, committing four turnovers, including a fumble returned for a Colts touchdown on the game's first play. Worse, while attempting to tackle Don Shinnick, who had scooped up the Bill Anderson fumble, Packers quarterback Bart Starr was lost to a shoulder injury and was gone for the afternoon. For the rest of the game, it would be backup Zeke Bratkowski's show, and he played OK, throwing for 248 yards.

In the end it came down to a controversial call that, in Baltimore at least, remains a source of fury. Trailing 10–7, the Packers drove down to the Colts 15 and in the final minute Don Chandler kicked a 22-yard field goal that, from his reaction, made it seem as though he had missed it to the right.

Instead, officials called it as the ball sailed high over the right upright, barely slipping inside the goalposts. The Colts were furious, convinced the kick had missed.

In the book *Facing the Green Bay Packers*, Matte remained adamant. "There is no way, no way that kick was good," he said. "I'll believe that forever."

Nonetheless, the Packers had tied the game and overtime ensued. Then with just over two minutes remaining, Chandler connected again, this time from 25 yards out, to give the Packers the conference title.

The championship game the following week on a sloppy Lambeau turf was almost anticlimactic. Despite featuring the NFL's best player in halfback Jim Brown, Cleveland could generate little offense. Quarterback Frank Ryan threw two interceptions and Brown rushed for just 50 yards on 12 carries.

Meanwhile Paul Hornung had a great game, rushing for 105 yards and a touchdown, and Jim Taylor added another 96 yards on the ground.

In the end Green Bay pounded out the 23–12 victory, the team's third title under Lombardi and ninth in franchise history.

But this was just the start. There was a fire burning deep in Lombardi at that time. He knew what he had in terms of talent and he knew he just might have a team for the ages. Knowing this, he planned to ride this train as far as it would go and he would push his players to the breaking point.

He had already led the Packers to back-to-back championships in 1961 and 1962. Now the thoughts began: Two titles in a row again? Why not? But three? Now that would be something. No team had ever won three in a row, and it would place the Packers, and himself, in a place no one else had ever visited.

And so it began.

In 1966 the goal would not, could not, change. To expect anything less than another championship would be doing a disservice to this team he had assembled and nurtured.

To win two straight would be tough enough, but the pro football landscape continued to shift and evolve. It was clear the rival American Football League wasn't going anywhere—it had money and credibility and fans behind it, and it was time for the two leagues to acknowledge that there was room for everyone.

So, in a decision that rocked the professional sports landscape, the NFL and AFL merged, and as part of that merger, a championship game would be played between the best team in the NFL and the champion of the AFL. It would be known as the "AFL-NFL World Championship Game," but in time it would evolve into the Super Bowl.

With this as the backdrop, the Packers went about the only job ahead of them—winning the conference. The world championship game? That was for another day and another time.

Green Bay rolled through the 1966 regular season, posting a 12–2 record with the only losses coming by a total of four points.

This team may have been every bit as good as the 1961 edition that most Packers of the time believe was the best ever assembled in Green Bay.

Bart Starr was in complete command of the offense and would be named the league's MVP that season. Jim Taylor had lost a step but was still a formidable fullback. Injuries had finally caught up to Paul Hornung and a pinched nerve bedeviled him all year to the point where he had all but decided to retire. But his place was taken by former first-round draft pick Elijah Pitts.

And the defense? It allowed barely 11 points a game, the best in the NFL, and forced 42 turnovers.

This was again a team built for the long haul (or as long as NFL careers would allow), but a new force was rising to the south and it was led by an old friend, and rival, of Vince Lombardi.

The Dallas Cowboys had been born out of chaos in 1960, not so subtly as the NFL's answer to the new American Football League.

Lamar Hunt, a prominent Texas businessman, had wanted to start an NFL franchise that year in Dallas, but the league rebuffed his efforts. So he joined a group that launched what would be called the American Football League and put a franchise in Dallas, known as the Texans.

Stunned by the move, the NFL decided that maybe a team in Dallas wasn't such a bad idea after all, and in January 1960 the NFL had its first expansion team. First known as the Steers and then the Rangers, by March the new team was finally called the Cowboys.

It was coached by Tom Landry, a bomber pilot in World War II and a former NFL defensive back, who cut his coaching teeth with the New York Giants as defensive coordinator. And the battles in practice with the team's offensive coordinator were legendary. That offensive coordinator, of course, was Vince Lombardi.

The two men respected each other's talent and approach to their jobs. To call them friends might have been a stretch because they were too different to be that close.

But each knew the other had the talent to one day run their own team, and now, in 1966, Landry's patience and devotion to his plan was paying off.

The Cowboys had become a force and the Packers knew they'd have to deal with this new, young, different approach.

And on January 1, 1967, at the Cotton Bowl in Dallas, the Packers and Cowboys would begin the dramatic dance that would eventually end on a frozen field in Green Bay a year later.

The Cowboys, who had rung up a 10–3–1 record to win the Eastern Conference title (it was also the franchise's first winning record since its formation seven years earlier), came into the NFL title game bursting with the kind of confidence that can only be found in youth. Indeed, none of the Dallas players had any championship game experience and only one player, linebacker Chuck Howley, was over the age of 30.

But they came in bristling with confidence anyway, because they saw in the Packers the team they wanted—they needed—to be when they grew up.

And as much as they respected their rivals and what they had accomplished over the years, they also saw in Green Bay a team that was starting to age, that was starting to lose its edge a little, and understood, perhaps prematurely, that their championship window was already starting to close. It was a new era in the NFL, the Cowboys believed, and they were the team to usher it in.

And it was a game to remember. In fact, this 1966 championship battle could well have found its place on the list of most important games in franchise history—if not for the game that would follow a year later.

The Packers jumped on the young Cowboys quickly as Elijah Pitts caught a 17-yard scoring pass from Starr on their first drive and then, just seconds later, Jim Grabowski scooped up Mel Renfro's fumbled kickoff and took it 18 yards to the end zone for another score. Just like that, 14–0.

But then something remarkable happened. While a number of the young Cowboys players were shaken by that start, quarterback Don Meredith wasn't. Meredith had been through the wars with this franchise already, foregoing law school and signing a five-year contract in 1960 before there was even an official franchise. Then he absorbed the beatings, both physical and mental, that come from playing with an expansion team where the losses pile up year after year.

But those years also made Meredith strong mentally and prepared him for the travails that would follow. And so it was after Green Bay jumped out to a 14–0 lead before the Dallas offense had even set foot on the field.

Meredith, in a story told by his center Dave Manders, gathered his shaken offense in the huddle and asked referee Tommy Bell for a timeout.

When Bell told Meredith he had to run a play first, Meredith looked at right tackle Ralph Neely, nodded to the stands near the 25-yard line, and said, "Hey Ralph, isn't that the girl you went out with last night? How was it?"

Manders said the huddle erupted in laughter and Meredith then turned to Bell again and said, "OK, Tom, we're ready to go."

The impromptu jab at Neely calmed down the offense, and by the end of the first quarter, the Cowboys had tied the game at 14–14.

On the third play of the second quarter, Starr threw a gorgeous 51-yard touchdown pass to Carroll Dale and Green Bay retook the lead. Dallas had its opportunities but could only manage two short field goals over the next two quarters, while Green Bay, thanks to two more Starr touchdown passes, eventually built a 34–20 lead with just over five minutes to play.

But the Cowboys finally found their spark, and Meredith connected with Frank Clark on a 61-yard scoring pass and got the ball again for one final effort to tie the game and send it to overtime.

The Cowboys moved all the way to the Packers' 2, but a costly false-start penalty on the Cowboys was devastating, and on fourth down from the Packers' 2, Meredith rolled to his right seeking a receiver in the end zone. But linebacker Dave Robinson roared in and enveloped Meredith, whose off-balance, wobbly pass was intercepted by Tom Brown in the end zone.

It wasn't always pretty and it wasn't as easy as it should have been, but the Packers had prevailed once again and secured their second straight league title and fourth under Lombardi.

But the job wasn't over because the rules had changed. Yes, the Packers had won yet another title, but there was now a new kid in town, and to secure the championship of professional football required one more step, one more game.

The AFL champion Kansas City Chiefs, after dispatching the Buffalo Bills in their title game, now awaited the Packers for the overall championship. It was played at the Los Angeles Coliseum on January 15, and as players revealed later, Lombardi had never been more nervous before a game than this one.

That's because he knew what was at stake for the NFL, for the Packers, and for the fans of Green Bay. Here were the Packers, the gold standard of professional football, who were expected to steamroll the interlopers from the rival league.

Lombardi viewed it as the classic no-win situation for his team—win the game and they had only done what was expected; lose and it would damage the reputation of the NFL and the proud Packers organization.

What followed, of course, was a surgical, relentless dissection of a Chiefs team that fought hard and had a few good moments but that, frankly, never had a chance.

Was this one of the most important games in Packers history? Many people would say yes because of how the Super Bowl has grown in importance and prestige and what it meant, especially to the NFL.

And while this game was certainly one of the most important in team history, the relative ease with which the Packers won has knocked it down the list. That's because the Packers beat the Chiefs 35–10 and barely broke a sweat doing it. In the end the NFL had proven its dominance and the AFL knew it had a long way to go.

Which brings us to perhaps the most important game in franchise history.

It was a long, circuitous route that got us to this point, but it was important to the overall narrative that what came before played a huge role in the game played December 31, 1967, a game that before it was even completed was already known as the "Ice Bowl."

There was more to this game than just the brutal weather, the players involved, the score, and the aftermath. It was a microcosm of an America being torn apart by social and political issues. It was a chance to view one pro football dynasty coming to an end and another beginning its rise to greatness. It was the end of a coaching career the likes of which may never be seen again, and it was an opportunity to watch a study in survival by men who were driven by the need to win.

And it was played at a time when America was convulsing with war protests and racial fissures and rampant disharmony to the point where nothing was as it used to be and everything was in the process of changing.

Were the Packers of 1967 the America of a bygone era, tired and out of step, and were the Cowboys the youthful and brimming future of an America to be? Sociologists can argue that one if they like. But suffice it to say that this game riveted a nation in ways very little else could at the time—if only to take their minds off what was, and what would happen down the road.

Was it great football played on the frozen field at Lambeau Field that day? No. The weather was as brutal as everyone who was there said it was. At least 10 players suffered some form of frostbite and three players suffered concussions when players wearing the flimsy plastic helmets of the day smacked their heads against the concrete-hard turf.

Offenses for both teams did next to nothing most of the day. Indeed, after the Packers jumped out to a quick 14–0 lead, they went nearly the next three quarters losing yardage.

The Cowboys, several of whom considered not even leaving the locker room before the game (but, of course, they did), actually seemed to adapt better to the conditions than the Packers and turned a spur-of-the-moment trick play into what was almost one of the most memorable in NFL history.

Then again, yes, it was great football because greatness isn't necessarily defined by style points or total yardage.

The Cowboys had come into the game confident and ready. The Packers had battled injuries all season and everyone, from the head coach on down, looked tired.

Bart Starr, the reigning NFL MVP, was bothered all season by a hand injury that forced him to miss two games and led to one of his worst seasons, in which he completed barely 50 percent of his passes and threw a career-high 17 interceptions.

And while much of the starting lineup remained the same from the previous seasons, important changes were coming.

The versatile Paul Hornung, bothered by a pinched nerve in his neck in 1966, was made available by the Packers in 1967 for the expansion draft to help fill the roster of the NFL's newest team, the New Orleans Saints. Hornung welcomed the decision because after what amounted to a wasted 1966 season, he believed he still had enough left in the tank to help the new team. Plus, after many off-season adventures, he had grown to love New Orleans.

But in the Saints' training camp that summer, he knew something wasn't right. Recurring numbness in his arms concerned him, and even though he'd been cleared by a doctor to play that season, he sought another opinion.

The answer wasn't what he had hoped to hear.

In his book, *The Paul Hornung Scrapbook*, he related this: "I'll never forget this. The doctor looked at the X-rays and said, 'You mean a doctor in Houston actually cleared you to play? Are you crazy?'"

The doctor laid it out in stark terms for him. Basically, Hornung's vertebrae no longer aligned properly and another hit could render him a paraplegic.

"That scared the hell out of me and I knew then that nothing was worth being paralyzed," he said. "I quit the next day."

A bigger blow was the loss of Hornung's backfield buddy, Jim Taylor, who played out his option with the Packers in 1966 and signed with the Saints, a return home for the Louisiana native who had played his college ball at LSU. He left after nine seasons as Green Bay's all-time leading rusher (8,207 yards, a record unbroken until Ahman Green 43 years later), and his 81 rushing touchdowns remains a team record.

As well, Fuzzy Thurston, Green Bay's longtime stalwart at left guard, had lost his starting job to the younger Gale Gillingham.

So change was coming. And add to that Lombardi's obsession with winning a third straight NFL championship.

"Lombardi never hid that fact," Packers' linebacker Dave Robinson said. "He wanted every player to know how important that was."

No team in NFL history had ever won three titles in a row, and Lombardi knew this Packers team had that ability. He drove the players relentlessly in an effort to make sure they took every step possible to secure that elusive goal.

But it would be a season where that goal seemed always just a little out of reach. It started with an opening-week tie with the Detroit Lions, which set the tone for a season where, due to injury and age, nothing came easily. Still, the Packers put together a 9–4–1 record despite losing their final two games of the regular season. It was good enough to claim the Central Division of the NFL's newly aligned Western Conference.

Waiting for them in the playoffs were the powerful Los Angeles Rams, owners of an NFL-best 11–1–2 record and a team many viewed as the team to beat that season.

"Everyone thought the Rams were the best team that season," Packers historian Cliff Christl said. "Even the Packers thought that."

But this was the postseason, and for the Packers, a light went on. This was what mattered. This was the next step toward NFL immortality and providing Lombardi with his crowning achievement, and every player knew it.

Guard Jerry Kramer, who chronicled the 1967 season with his tape recorder and collaborated with author Dick Schaap for the best-selling book *Instant Replay*, recalled how the playoffs seemed to spark Lombardi.

"It's as if he'd been saving himself all year long, to get this extracur-ricular stuff (also known as the regular season) out of the way and now it looks like he's come to life," Kramer said in a recording with Schaap. "It's like he'd been lying dormant for 14 weeks and now he's coming to life. I remember he talked the week before the Rams game about St. Paul's Epistle and that there are many runners in the race but only one prize. So he said let's run the race to win. Then he smiled and said, 'Paul was a hell of a guy before the lions got him.'"

The game was played before a full house at Milwaukee County Stadium and in 13-degree weather. But the Rams came on the field with no cold-weather gear, and their coach, George Allen, wore a short-sleeved shirt and proclaimed, "This is Rams weather."

"We thought he was crazy," Kramer said.

Said safety Doug Hart, "We knew they were freaked out by the weather."

The Packers overcame four turnovers, shook off a 7–0 deficit after the first quarter, and took command of the game thanks to a rookie running back nicknamed "The Roadrunner."

Travis Williams was Green Bay's fourth-round draft pick that year from Arizona State, an acknowledgment from Lombardi the general manager that it was time to turn the page from the "Thunder and Lightning" team of Taylor and Hornung.

In that rookie season, Williams was more noted for his prowess as a kick returner. Indeed, he set an NFL record by averaging 41 yards per return and scoring four touchdowns.

Packers tight end Marv Fleming told Christl once that all anyone on the kickoff had to do was occupy his defender for a split second.

"And Travis was gone," he said. "He was that quick."

But Williams had gotten little opportunity to show his skills as a running back, first backing up Elijah Pitts and then Donny Anderson. Then an injury knocked Pitts out of the playoff game and Williams got his opportunity.

Early in the second quarter, after a great punt return from Tom Brown, Williams took a handoff from Starr on the next play and blasted through the Rams' vaunted "Fearsome Foursome" for a momentum-shifting 46-yard touchdown run. The Packers took it from there.

Starr completed 17 of 23 passes for 222 yards with a second-quarter TD pass to Boyd Dowler. Chuck Mercein, unemployed and planning in mere hours to sign with the Washington Redskins before Lombardi called, scored on a six-yard run, and Williams ran in for his second touchdown of the day to seal an impressive 28–7 win.

Williams had the game of his life, rushing for 88 yards on 18 carries, and Anderson added another 52 yards on the ground. Meanwhile, the Packers defense was as it ever was—holding Rams quarterback Roman Gabriel to 11 completions out of 31 attempts for 186 yards and one interception.

The defense held the Rams to just 217 total yards, and despite four Green Bay turnovers, allowed just one score. It was a sign that the Packers, despite a season of uncharacteristic inconsistency, were ready for prime time.

Waiting next was a familiar foe, the Dallas Cowboys, winners of the Capitol Division of the Eastern Conference. The Cowboys had made their playoff statement, too, blasting the Cleveland Browns 52–14 in their divisional-round game.

So the rematch from 1966 was set—the Green Bay Packers would host the Dallas Cowboys at Lambeau Field. And the weather forecast from the Thursday prior to the game was calling for a cold, clear day. Temperatures in the 20s but nothing unusual for early winter in Wisconsin.

On his weekly TV show a few days before the game, Vince Lombardi smiled and said, "I'm glad the game is in Green Bay. The weather's supposed to be beautiful."

The day before the game, the Cowboys ran through a quick practice and they agreed. For this time of year in this part of the country, they could not have expected more.

"It was cold but we were expecting it," said Cowboys halfback Dan Reeves. "It was actually pretty comfortable. And we were ready. We had learned a lot from the year before [the 31–24 loss to the Packers at the

Cotton Bowl] and we knew what we needed to do. We really thought, we knew, we were the better team."

But that night, while the Packers and Cowboys and the 50,000 fans expected at Lambeau Field the next day slept, an unseen and unexpected cold front swooped in from Canada and changed everything.

This is a book about stories, and some of the best can be found, and heard, from the morning of December 31, 1967.

There is the story of Cowboys quarterback Don Meredith receiving his wakeup call from the receptionist at the Appleton, Wisconsin, hotel 20 miles from Green Bay where the team was staying. The story, according to a 50-year anniversary article in the *Milwaukee Journal Sentinel*, goes that the call went to Meredith and he heard the words, "Howdy doody Packer backer, it's 20 below." Meredith reportedly said, "20 below what?" and the receptionist said with a laugh, "Just step outside, sir."

Reeves was incredulous as well, believing he had heard it wrong before stepping outside and realizing he had not.

The Packers were not immune. Several players emerged from their homes, stunned by what had enveloped them, and could not start their cars due to the cold. Instead, they would call taxis or neighbors to bring them to the stadium.

All-Pro linebacker Dave Robinson remembers thinking, "*This is crazy.*"

It was so cold, there was consideration about postponing the game, and even some Cowboys players believed it would be too brutal to contest a game of this importance. But NFL Commissioner Pete Rozelle, ensconced warmly in Oakland, California, for the AFL Championship Game, made it clear that postponing the game was not an option.

So one of the great human sports dramas would take place whether the players liked it or not.

Ironically, Packers coach Vince Lombardi had invested thousands of dollars of the Packers' money in a state-of-the-art heating coil system under Lambeau Field for just such an emergency.

Installed prior to the season, Lombardi was as proud of this new innovation as he would have been showing off a new grandchild.

Operated inside Lambeau Field, the belief was that this system would warm the field on especially cold Wisconsin days and provide great footing for both teams to perform.

Reporters from those days would remark how Lombardi would show them how it worked and how important it would be, and he beamed with pride at how clever an idea it was. And it was indeed. Except someone forgot to mention the science of condensation to the coach.

The night before the game, the field was covered with a tarpaulin to protect it, and the heating coil system was turned on. Overnight, the heat created a layer of moisture on the warm field and when the tarp was removed the next morning, the moisture froze, turning the field slippery. As the day went on, the temperature dropped and the wind picked up, turning a slippery field to solid ice. By the end of the game, it was all but impossible for either team to gain anything resembling decent footing, which, naturally, impacted the quality of the play.

It also enraged Lombardi, who saw his pride-and-joy (and expensive) heating system betray him and damage his team's chances of winning that coveted third straight title.

But in truth, the weather helped no one and hurt everyone, including the nearly 50,000 fans who still showed up to watch their Packers.

Gil Brandt, at the time the Cowboys' director of player personnel (and a Wisconsin native), recalled in the book *Ice Bowl '67* how he went onto the field an hour before the game and saw few fans in the stands. He thought, just maybe, even Packers fans had the good sense to stay home when the temperature was headed toward a windchill of 30 below and watch it on TV from the warm comfort of their living rooms.

He thought wrong.

He went back into the Cowboys' locker room, came out again 10 minutes before the game, and the stands were full.

"It was amazing," he said.

In the end the game was listed as a sellout, though there were certainly empty seats. And the myth began to grow about this game, and for years to come, and forever after, generations of Packers fans would claim that they were on hand, freezing and cheering and living and dying with their heroes, to watch what unfolded on this treacherous Sunday afternoon.

There was something about this game that everyone knew, almost instinctively, that by the time it was over, the NFL, the Cowboys, and the Packers would all be changed for good.

Dan Reeves, who died in December 2021, was an integral part of this game who would go on to win 201 games and reach four Super Bowls as a head coach. He knew even then that this was a kind of game he likely would never be a part of again.

"I think it revealed the inner character of everyone involved," he said in *Ice Bowl '67*.

Reeves was one of many players, from both sidelines, who questioned the sanity of playing the game. But they all knew it was their job to compete since this, after all, was the NFL title game.

But the fans? The reason for their appearance mystified the Cowboys especially, who looked in the stands at the bundled masses enveloped in clouds of steam and simply shook their heads.

Cowboys running back Walt Garrison remembers turning to fellow back Don Perkins and saying simply, "These people are crazy."

And what they saw was not so much superbly executed football, but the will and stamina and guts and determination of two teams intent on not letting the elements dictate the game to them.

In the end fans saw their Packers find something deep down that many of them weren't sure was even there and pull out a victory that makes this, without question, the most important game in Packers history.

It is a great story to tell that this was a battle between the NFL that was and the NFL that would be. And in some ways, it is true.

The Packers of Vince Lombardi had won on pinpoint precision and belief in a system and by understanding that not giving 100 percent on every play for their coach was a dereliction of duty.

The Cowboys of Tom Landry were different. By this point in their evolution as a franchise, the Cowboys clearly had more talent than the Packers. They were stronger, faster, and younger, and they brimmed with a confidence that was only slightly diminished by the close title loss to Green Bay the season before at the Cotton Bowl.

This was a confident, athletic team. But the one thing they lacked, the one thing that could not be taught, was how to win in tough situations. That could only be learned through rigorous and sometimes painful experience.

And a forgotten point in this game was the fact that many of the Packers already knew that this would be Lombardi's final game at Lambeau Field as Green Bay's head coach. Lombardi had told several players, but most knew their coach so well that they knew what was coming. And there was an emotion at work here that no amount of game preparation could overcome.

Jerry Kramer knew. He had developed a special bond with Lombardi over the years to the point that in the decades after he left football, he carried the gospel of Lombardi wherever he went.

"He changed my life," Kramer has often said.

Another story, and one that Kramer has told many hundreds of times over the years, is a story that speaks volumes:

"I'd had a really bad practice one day and Coach was all over me. I'd jump offsides and he was in my face and 'Mister, the concentration period of a college student is five minutes; for a high school student it's three minutes, and for a kindergartner it's 30 seconds. So where does that put you?' So I was sitting at my locker feeling lower than duck s——and believing that I was never going to make it in the NFL. So Coach comes up to me, tousles my hair, and tells me, 'Young man, one of these days you're going to be the best guard in football.' You wouldn't believe what that did for me. He wanted everything from you and you wanted to give it to him."

So when Lombardi intimated to Kramer that this would be it with the Packers, Kramer wasn't necessarily surprised. But he was driven. And he made sure his teammates were as well.

Officially, the temperature at game time was 17 below zero with a windchill of 45 below. The numbers have changed over the years, but as Reeves often said, "Once it got that cold, did it really matter?"

Eventually, the game got under way, and after an initial Dallas possession and punt, the Packers got down to business. Thanks to two Cowboys penalties, Green Bay skated 82 yards on 14 plays as Bart Starr completed four of five passes for 52 yards, including an eight-yard scoring pass to Boyd Dowler.

At the opening of the second quarter, the Packers struck again as Starr hit Dowler for a 43-yard touchdown and, in rapidly deteriorating weather conditions, what seemed a nearly insurmountable 14–0 lead.

But as the temperature got colder, the Packers froze up, too, and in a staggering display of Cowboys defense and Packers futility, over the next two and a half quarters, Green Bay's offense managed to run just 30 offensive plays, losing nine yards along the way. As well, Starr was sacked seven times, including one that led to a fumble return for a Dallas TD.

Robinson recalled years later, "I had lost faith in the offense."

Meanwhile, the Cowboys had embraced the conditions, understood they had the defending two-time NFL champs on the ropes, and were doing their best to put them away.

Finally, on the first play of the fourth quarter and down 14–10, the Cowboys went to their rarely used bag of tricks. On second down from the 50-yard line, Meredith pitched the ball to Reeves, a former quarterback himself, and as he swept left he saw safety Tom Brown move up to close him down. Reeves stopped and lofted a pass to a wide-open Lance Rentzel for the stunning touchdown.

"We really thought that was going to be the decisive score," Reeves recalled.

And indeed, the Cowboys defense was playing so well that Green Bay continued to sputter on its next two series. The legend of the Dallas "Doomsday Defense" was asserting its will and an aging, demoralized Packers team was taking the full brunt.

But after a Cowboys' drive stalled and Willie Wood returned the ensuing punt to the Green Bay 32 with 4:54 to play, something unexpected and remarkable happened: the Packers remembered who they were and how they got there.

In later years Starr said that as he entered the huddle for that pivotal drive, he was planning to say something inspirational. But he changed his mind once he looked around at his teammates.

"There was nothing I needed to say," he said in the book *Game of My Life*. "All I knew was that every guy was looking at me and I saw something in their eyes that made me realize we were going to get this done."

That final drive has been analyzed and scrutinized in the decades since. It was a desperate drive borne of the realization that there was no more time and no more opportunities to be great. It would happen here and it would happen now or it would not happen at all.

These final 12 plays orchestrated on a field that was now totally ice was not a thing of beauty. There was stumbling and sliding and lunging, as though some great wounded beast was lurching toward safety. But it was effective.

It may be the most famous drive in NFL history. And what made it even more compelling was that it made a hero, if only briefly, of a journeyman running back from Yale who had signed with the Packers only weeks earlier.

Prior to that, Chuck Mercein had played sparingly with the New York Giants, who released him at midseason, and he was marking time playing semi-pro ball while waiting, he hoped, for another call from the NFL. He was planning to sign with the Washington Redskins when Lombardi called and asked if he wanted to join the Packers.

His response? "Are you kidding?" Mercein was in Green Bay the next day, and on this last day of 1967, his name would become known to every Packers fan forever after.

His final statistics for the game were nothing to notice. He carried the ball six times and gained 20 yards and caught two passes for 22 yards. But the yards were crucial and came when they were needed most. Without them, the Cowboys very likely would have been playing in the second Super Bowl.

The drive encompassed 68 yards over the final four minutes of the game, and in the minds of many longtime NFL observers, it was one of the greatest ever for a number of reasons.

"Everyone knew exactly what was at stake," Starr recalled.

First, the circumstances. Second, the weather/field conditions. Third, for a team that had struggled offensively most of the day, it came out of nowhere. Fourth, it was a drive put together by an aging, injured team and accomplished, in many respects, for their coach, who had given them so much.

"That drive for me was probably the most complete concentration effort in that period of time that I've ever given to football," said left tackle Bob Skoronski years later on a tape for *Jerry Kramer's Inside the Locker Room*. "I knew full well we were either going to do it or we weren't and I thought about ways they couldn't beat me. You knew we couldn't blow anything. It was a terrifically concentrated and high effort as the game has ever demanded of me. There was no thought of not succeeding."

Paul Hornung was standing on the Packers sideline in street clothes, having already retired but wanting to be a part of what was happening because even he sensed this was the end of something truly special.

"I stood next to Lombardi the entire game and he'd ask me if I saw any plays that might work, to let him know," Hornung recalled in *The Paul Hornung Scrapbook*. "But I never saw anything. Besides, it was so cold I probably could have told him anything. I don't care what anybody says today, it has never been colder than it was that day. That game should have been postponed. I have no idea why it wasn't."

Hornung was next to Lombardi when Bart Starr called the Packers' final timeout with 16 seconds left to play and Green Bay less than a yard from a game-winning touchdown.

The Packers had gotten there thanks, first, to a 19-yard pass from Starr to Mercein to the Dallas 11 and then an eight-yard Mercein run to the three.

"I still think that was the best call of the entire drive and the best call I ever made," Starr related years later. "It was perfect timing and if the field had been better, Mercein would have scored."

Anderson's two-yard gain set up a first-and-goal, and a touchdown seemed inevitable—until it didn't.

On the next two plays, standard handoffs right up the middle (a staple of the Packers offense), Anderson could not gain any traction on the icy field and gained nothing. Now on third down and with no time-outs remaining, this would be Green Bay's last chance as there wouldn't be enough time to run another play.

Starr stood on the sidelines and spoke with Lombardi about what should come next. It was a conversation every Packers fan, and probably every Cowboys fan, knows by heart.

Analytical and unemotional, Starr told his already-iconic head coach that the field was simply too icy for the backs to get their footing and another handoff would be pointless. He was already under center, he told Lombardi, and could take the snap and lunge into the end zone if his linemen could make critical blocks.

Lombardi's response? "Then run it and let's get the hell out of here."

"I was laughing all the way back to the huddle," Starr said.

It was a call many of the Cowboys' defenders expected, but not head coach and defensive genius Tom Landry. The Packers had not run a quarterback sneak all season and the audaciousness of doing so at that spot, in that situation, made no sense to the analytical coach.

He expected Starr to roll out and look for an open receiver in the end zone, and if he couldn't find one, to throw the ball away. That would have set up a short field goal to tie the game and send it into overtime—which no one wanted. Besides, even a short field goal at that time of day and on that field was no certainty.

"[The sneak] was not a good call, but now it's a great call," a devastated Landry said in a postgame interview.

That short plunge into the end zone has been analyzed ad nauseum since the day it happened, and it was a textbook example of how well the Packers executed everything they did.

And it began with deception in the Packers huddle. Only Starr and Lombardi knew the sneak was coming, and when Starr called the play "31 Wedge" and asked his linemen if they could get their footing for one more wedge play, it was assumed the ball would go to Mercein.

On the other side of the line, Cowboys Hall of Fame defensive tackle Bob Lilly considered calling a timeout of their own so they could dig in for better footing for the sneak they were sure was coming.

He recalled in the book *Ice Bowl '67* how he wanted to have the Cowboys' equipment manager, Jack Eskridge, come out on the field with a screwdriver and dig a trench for the lineman to get better footing.

"But we didn't do it," he said. "We should have, but I don't think any of us were going to get to Bart anyway. It was a great call."

The rest, as they say, is history. Center Ken Bowman snapped the ball to Starr and fired out, along with right guard Jerry Kramer, to block defensive tackle Jethro Pugh. The double team created just enough of a crease for Starr to slip through and across the goal line.

The Dallas defenders maintain to this day that Kramer got out of his three-point stance ahead of the snap and should have been flagged for offsides, which in today's NFL parlance is called a false start.

"Of course he was offsides," Lilly said.

It didn't matter. Starr had scored what would go down as one of the most famous touchdowns in NFL history, capping one of the greatest drives in NFL history, accomplished by one of the greatest teams in NFL history.

And before it ended with a harmless incomplete pass from quarterback Don Meredith to wide receiver Bob Hayes, the game was already finding its way into the pantheon of all-time epic American sporting events.

Ironically, many of the nation's top sportswriters and columnists didn't make the trip to Green Bay due to the weather or other assignments, so the reaction came secondhand and by virtue of watching the game on TV. But the reaction was the same: everyone had just seen a game the likes of which they may never see again, and as the reactions rolled in, it became clear even to the Packers and Cowboys that they had participated in something truly special.

Said Dan Reeves ruefully: "It's the only game I played in that has a name attached to it."

And so it would forever.

And that would have been a dramatic and thunderous period to place on the NFL's 1967 season, except that there was one more game left—and it was one the Packers were not exactly brimming with enthusiasm to participate in. Indeed, two weeks after literally leaving pieces of themselves on the Lambeau Field ice rink, the Packers would play in the second AFL-NFL Championship Game, in perhaps as anticlimactic a title game as was ever played.

The dynastic Packers had just beaten what may have been the NFL's best team in a game that was already entering into the realm of the mythic. And now Green Bay had to travel to Miami to play the AFL champion Oakland Raiders?

When asked after the Ice Bowl about the looming matchup in Florida, the smile disappeared from Starr's face. "I don't even want to think about that," he said.

But eventually, he would, and the result would allow the Packers to move from the realm of great NFL teams to a pedestal where no one else resided.

CHAPTER SIX

"WE'RE BEING ASKED ONE MORE TIME TO DO THIS"

PACKERS 33, OAKLAND RAIDERS 14

JANUARY 14, 1968

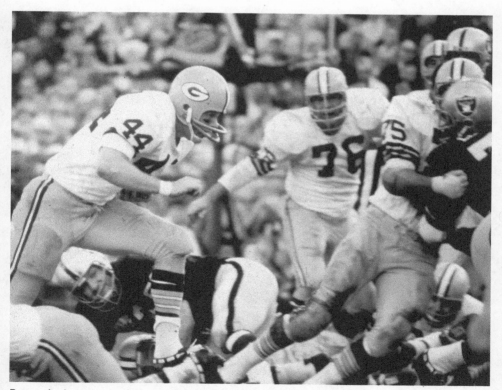

Donny Anderson scores against the Raiders during Super Bowl II at the Orange Bowl.
AP FILE PHOTO

IT HAD LURKED BELOW THE SURFACE ALL SEASON. IT WAS WHAT DROVE Vince Lombardi to what some players viewed as a maniacal obsession and it was, very likely, what eventually led to the decision that would alter the Packers franchise forever.

His Packers had won two straight NFL championships, including the first Super Bowl the year before. But now he wanted, he needed, more. Lombardi knew he had created the closest thing to a dynasty that the NFL was ever likely to see, winning titles in 1961, 1962, 1965, and 1966. And that was great.

But no team in the league's history had won three in a row, and that was what separated his Packers from a spot on Mount Olympus. And since training camp that summer, Lombardi's only goal was to somehow inspire his slowly aging team to dig down one more time for that elusive prize. And through a difficult season of injury and inconsistency, his Packers were right there on the brink of accomplishing what few thought was possible.

The already iconic Ice Bowl win two weeks earlier over the Cowboys that had secured Green Bay's third straight NFL title had taken its toll—especially mentally—on his team.

They were worn out and banged up physically and wrung out emotionally after already winning what many of the players considered the *real* championship.

But what awaited was Super Bowl II in Miami against the AFL's top team, the Oakland Raiders, who came in with a 13–1 record and wanted the respect the league was still seeking and would only get with a Super Bowl title.

And while several Packers viewed the Raiders as little more than an annoyance, the fact was these Raiders could play.

They had destroyed the Houston Oilers, 40–7, in the AFL title game, and they featured a strong, fast, nasty defense—not unlike the Cowboys—that had given Green Bay so much trouble. The Cowboys "D" had what was dubbed the "Doomsday Defense"; the Raiders called their defense "Eleven Angry Men." The Packers defense? It had no nickname. It just played at a high level every snap, every game.

On offense Oakland featured a great story in quarterback Daryle Lamonica, who had come to the Raiders in a trade with Buffalo that off-season after four seasons of mostly languishing on the bench with the Bills. Now free to run a new, wide-open offense, Lamonica proceeded to throw for more than 3,000 yards and 30 touchdowns, leading the highest-scoring offense in the AFL, earning him the league MVP and the superb nickname "The Mad Bomber."

So all the pieces were in place for a great game with circumstances not unlike the Ice Bowl. The Packers had gotten no younger in the two weeks since the NFL title game, and their enthusiasm for this second straight NFL-AFL championship match was something less than overwhelming.

Meanwhile, the Raiders brought a more mature but typically ebullient AFL attitude toward this next great opportunity for the league to prove its worth to the more dominant NFL. They were younger, faster, stronger, and likely more motivated for the game than the exhausted Packers. Just like the Dallas Cowboys had come into Green Bay two weeks earlier.

So, yes, it should have been a good game but, once again, it was not.

Lombardi had been concerned that the physical Raiders would gain confidence and swagger if they could come out early and dominate the game.

"Don't play their game," Lombardi told his team in what would prove to be his final pregame talk as head coach of the Green Bay Packers. "Keep your poise."

He also added this in relation to an unprecedented third straight championship: "You're a good football team, a powerful football team, and you're a championship team. No one has ever done what you can do today, and all the glory of everything you've had is going to be small in comparison to winning this. Boys, if I were you, I'd be proud of that."

One of the Packers team captains, defensive end Willie Davis, also appealed to his teammates.

"We need to do this to make one statement of certainty that the Green Bay Packers have been the best football team in the business," Davis relayed on the Kramer tape. "We're being asked one more time to do this. And I'm not ready to explain how we'd lose this."

Enough said. On the first offensive play, Packers linebacker Ray Nitschke knifed through the Oakland line and upended Raiders running back Hewritt Dixon. The Packers had made their statement: the Raiders weren't ready for the bright lights just yet.

In front of a record TV viewing audience and national media from around the country, the Packers did what they always did when they had to—they played smart, disciplined, strategic football and they dispatched the Raiders, 33–14.

The Packers defense held the Raiders' potent offense to a season-low 293 total yards and forced three turnovers. Don Chandler kicked four field goals and Bart Starr threw for 202 yards and a touchdown and earned his second straight Super Bowl MVP award.

If there was any drama, it was Lombardi's decision on who would start at running back. It was assumed by everyone, including the Packers, that Chuck Mercein, who had played so well in the postseason, especially in the Ice Bowl, would get the call. But Lombardi, always the master manipulator, had a hunch.

In pregame warmups he went up to Ben Wilson, who had not played at all in the Ice Bowl and had really not contributed much to the effort all season since coming to the Packers in a long-forgotten trade that summer. Asked by Lombardi how he felt, Wilson said, "Fine." And that was that. Wilson slipped into the backfield along with Donny Anderson while a stunned Mercein stood on the sidelines. Mercein, the hero of the most important game in Packers history, did play but carried the ball just once for no yardage.

After the game, Mercein just shrugged. "You don't argue with the decisions Vince Lombardi makes," he said.

Wilson would go on to rush for a game-high 62 yards on 17 carries, and that was with missing the fourth quarter because of a lost contact lens. And that would be the highlight of his Packers career when, after complications from off-season knee surgery, Wilson never played for the Packers or in the NFL again.

As the Orange Bowl clock wound down, Vince Lombardi, led by perhaps the coach's greatest supporter in Jerry Kramer, was carried off the field in triumph and relief and glory.

"I had said at halftime to the rest of the team that we should play the last 30 minutes for the old man," Kramer recalled on more than a few occasions. "And I thought it was appropriate that we carry him off the field after the game. It was a tribute to him. All he said when we were carrying him off was, 'OK boys, let's go to the locker room.'"

It was yet another dominant performance by the Packers on the biggest stage, but several Packers simply shrugged off the rather perfunctory dissection.

"I thought I was ready for this one," Forrest Gregg, the Packers veteran offensive tackle, told *Sports Illustrated* afterward. "When I got out there, I just did not have the zip I had against Dallas and Los Angeles. It was mechanical. It's been a long, long season."

Linebacker Lee Roy Caffey couldn't disagree with his teammate, telling *SI*, "It's tough to get up again when you've been on the stick for two big games. I know we did not play as well as we have. We made mistakes we don't make in most games. But I guess it turned out all right, didn't it?"

It did and would mark the end of an era never to be seen again. Three straight championships. A place in NFL and American sports history. A franchise for the ages whose name would reverberate throughout the decades as the greatest dynasty the league had ever seen.

And the Packers were exhausted. This season of tribulation and eventual success had wrung them dry—from longtime veterans who had seen all this before to the rookie who was still figuring everything out. As Forrest Gregg had said, it had been a long, long season.

But for no one had it been longer than Lombardi. He had coached the Packers for nine seasons, and each one had been harder than the last. He had put everything into making the Packers the best team in football, and he had succeeded, probably more often than even he had imagined.

Under Lombardi's withering glare, the Packers had won five NFL championships. They had set the standard for how to play the game with intelligence, passion, and attention to detail. The expectations had been crushing and they had been self-induced. For Lombardi, losing football games felt worse than the adulation of winning football games, and there was something wrong with that formula.

But more to the point, everyone, from inside the organization to the casual fan, knew that time and age had won yet again.

"After that second Super Bowl, this was the end of an era and I think everyone knew it," center Ken Bowman said.

There are a number of reasons why this game belongs on the list of most important in team history—not the least of which was it cemented the Packers as the greatest team of the 1960s. But more to the point, it was an understanding by everyone involved that this was the end and they went out as they had come in—as winners. It was a bittersweet and moving time.

Of course, the Packers' golden era officially ended barely three weeks later when Lombardi confirmed what many players had already suspected.

In what Lombardi would admit later was an impetuous, and probably major, mistake, on February 1, 1968, a press conference was held and Lombardi announced he was stepping down as head coach. There was no list of potential replacements for who would take over in what many considered a no-win position, because Lombardi hand-picked his longtime defensive coordinator, Phil Bengtson, as his successor. He did not discuss it with the Packers' powerful executive committee, which normally had the say over who would get such an important job. But they understood only too well that this was Lombardi and what the coach wanted, the coach got.

Lombardi remained as general manager, but it was a situation doomed from the start.

The old coach was miserable in his abbreviated role. Bengtson, who had never been a head coach before, approached the game and his players in a far different manner than Lombardi. And observers at the time recalled how Lombardi would walk by himself, far from the practice field but close enough to watch what was happening, his hands clasped behind his back, looking down, wondering if he'd made the right decision.

He knew fairly quickly that he had not. He made the decision when he was still emotionally and physically frayed from a difficult season. He should have waited, gathered his thoughts, talked to people, been more organized—all the things he always preached to his players. But he had not and now it was eating him alive.

And it did not help that the Packers, now gaining speed on the downhill slope from greatness, were struggling on the field. After a season-opening win over the Eagles in 1968, the Packers lost three of their next four games on the way to a 6–7–1 record and a third-place finish in a mediocre Central Division. It was Green Bay's first losing season since 1958 and signaled that the ever-evolving NFL was doing it again.

Sure, many of the same pieces that had been in place for the three championships were still there, but everything seemed and felt different. Bart Starr was hurt again. The offense sputtered and the defense, long the centerpiece of these dominant Packers teams, was starting to fray.

"I think we lost our heartbeat a little," veteran wide receiver Boyd Dowler recalled on Kramer's tape. "It was a case of it wasn't our time anymore. Our time had passed."

And watching it all was the old lion. Would anything have been appreciably different with these Packers if Lombardi was still prowling the sidelines? Maybe. But as good a coach and motivator as he was, he could not have stopped time in its tracks, and that was the major issue.

Jerry Kramer would retire after the 1968 season, Willie Davis after the 1969 season, and Willie Wood after the 1971 season. In 1972 Herb Adderley was traded to the Dallas Cowboys, Dave Robinson was sent to the Washington Redskins, and Bart Starr and Ray Nitschke retired. Forrest Gregg retired after both the 1969 and 1970 seasons but changed his mind each time. Then in 1971 he was waived by new Packers coach Dan Devine and signed with the Cowboys, where he was part of another Super Bowl winner.

So, as it is with all things, time was slowly but surely eroding the greatest team in NFL history. And in 1968 Lombardi observed, powerless to stop it.

It is another well-known story that during this mediocre season, the Packers soundproofed the GM's box in Lambeau Field that was located next to the press box. The reason? Team officials did not want the media listening as Lombardi roared and screamed and fulminated at what he was witnessing on the field.

It was clear Lombardi was not finished coaching. He wanted back in, but he wanted back in on his terms. He had already struck up conversations through that year with Washington Redskins owner Edward Bennett Williams, who saw in Lombardi the savior for his moribund franchise that Packers officials had seen in him 10 years earlier.

So in a process that took weeks of negotiations and more than a few harsh words, the Packers released Lombardi from his contract and allowed him to sign as head coach, general manager, and part owner of the Redskins.

And if an era had not ended before that, it surely had by this point.

In his one season with the Redskins in 1969, Lombardi again weaved his magic, leading Washington, which had not had a winning season since 1955, to a 7–5–2 mark.

But by the time the 1970 season opened, cancer had taken Lombardi's life and, aside from a brief resurrection in 1972, the Green Bay Packers would find themselves in a two-decade journey through mediocrity, controversy, and, unbelievably, a return to irrelevancy.

Jerry Kramer recounted a story in the book *The Green Bay Packers All-Time All-Stars* that spoke volumes about what had transpired in Green Bay over that remarkable time period.

It was his final season in 1968 and in the home finale against the Baltimore Colts at Lambeau Field, a last-minute fumble signaled a loss and the realization that the title defense was officially over.

"I'm thinking, 'We're done. We're not going to the playoffs. An era is over,'" Kramer said. "I come off the field and there's a smattering of applause from the crowd and I'm thinking, 'It's over, we lost.'

But more and more people were standing up and they gave us a five-minute standing ovation. And then I thought, 'They know it's over and they understand.' It was a thank-you for so many wonderful years. That impressed me. It made me understand Packers fans a lot better. It's pretty special. We knew that was the end of something, and the beginning, and that's when I knew it wasn't really over. It was the bond between the team and the fans, and I knew that would live forever."

That bond, of course, would be tested time and again for more than 20 years as Green Bay descended back into a period that many never thought would appear again.

For 24 seasons, from 1968 to 1991, the Packers would see winning seasons just four times, reach the playoffs three times, and win exactly one playoff game.

And now a threat resounded through every other NFL team for players who did not perform up to expectations: "Get better or we'll trade you to Green Bay." It was a fate worse than death.

Bob Harlan, who joined the Packers in 1971 as a public relations director and in 1991 was team president, had watched this for far too long. It was time for a change. Not cosmetic change to appease the fan base but radical, systemic, foundational change that would change the culture and rock the foundation of not only Packers fans but the NFL.

That's when he contacted Ron Wolf and asked what he thought about coming to the Packers.

CHAPTER SEVEN

"WE'VE PUT OUR FUTURE IN HIS HANDS"

PACKERS 28, DETROIT LIONS 24

JANUARY 8, 1994

Mike Holmgren and Brett Favre share a quiet moment following the Packers' 1994 wild-card playoff victory over the Lions in the Pontiac Silverdome. AP/VERNON BIEVER

On this list of the most important games in franchise history, perhaps the one that might raise the eyebrows of Packers fans is this one. But upon further reflection and analysis, this was a sneaky vital game because it was the one that set up everything that was to come and what would develop into the next golden age of Green Bay Packers football.

This come-from-behind playoff victory, Green Bay's first in 12 seasons and first away from the comfy environs of Wisconsin since 1966, was a tantalizing precursor of what was to come for the Packers.

It was the game that told dubious fans that, yes, this heralded head coach from California, Mike Holmgren, in just his second season, might know what he was doing after all. It told them that the general manager put in place three years earlier to change everything, Ron Wolf, was doing just that.

And it told everyone who was paying attention that this wild, exciting, breathtakingly inconsistent, and entertaining young quarterback might well be the answer to so many questions.

"We've put our future in his hands," Wolf told the *Milwaukee Journal Sentinel* after the win over the Lions. "If that young quarterback read everything written about him, I don't know if he'd make an appearance other than in disguise."

No doubt, the legend of Brett Favre was already taking root and it would only grow larger as the years went by. But there was more.

This was the game that allowed the Packers, as a franchise, to peek over the hill and glimpse just what might lie ahead. And it was a sight to see.

But it was a long, painful journey to get to this feeling of anticipation, and, indeed, it would not have seemed so thrilling if the previous two decades of Packers teams had not teetered between mediocrity and embarrassment. It is truly the case, for the Packers of this time, that you don't appreciate the highs without first experiencing the lows.

And for the Packers, after carrying Vince Lombardi out of the Orange Bowl on their shoulders after winning Super Bowl II in January 1968, very little had gone right.

In almost a whirlwind, an exhausted and ill Lombardi stepped down as head coach and gave the job to his dutiful and loyal defensive coordinator Phil Bengtson.

A capable coordinator and nice guy, Bengtson was in over his head from the start, and in his three forgettable seasons, the Packers went 20–21–1, losing almost as many games in that time frame as Lombardi lost in his nine seasons.

The great players who had made the Packers an NFL dynasty in the decade were retiring or were traded. Lombardi, who had known almost immediately that quitting had been a mistake, prowled the sidelines as general manager depressed and anxious. After a year of agony, he convinced the Packers to release him from his contract so he could coach again with the Washington Redskins. But a year later he was dead, and the Packers felt that loss to their core.

It would get no better as the years went by. Bengtson was replaced by Dan Devine, who had one winning season and a single playoff appearance in four seasons. Dour and unimaginative, Devine alienated players and fans alike, and when he left, quietly, to return to the college ranks and coach at Notre Dame, no one shed a tear.

Then, in an effort to recapture their past glory, Green Bay reached back and hired a thoroughly unprepared Bart Starr as head coach. Admired to the point of reverence for his 16 years as the Packers' quarterback and the face of the dynasty, Starr had never coached anywhere in anything before, and it showed.

Because he was Bart Starr, he was given a far longer rope than most coaches even back then would have received. And while the consensus was that over his nine seasons Starr had become a solid, even a good, NFL head coach, the final results were nowhere to be seen. His teams, by and large, were exciting on offense and horrendous on defense, resulting in a final record of 52–76–3 that included one trip to the postseason and one playoff victory. Still, when the Packers' executive board fired him after the 1983 season, players and fans alike were stunned.

"You just didn't fire Bart Starr," remarked one player at the time, though it was a thought on every player's mind.

But they did fire Bart Starr, and if there was ever a rock bottom for the Packers franchise, it may well have been the five years that followed, first under another former Packers great player, Forrest Gregg, and then the circus that followed and eventually led to the hiring of Lindy Infante.

On the field, problems were bad enough as Green Bay descended into undisciplined play that was hallmarked by the rivalry with the Chicago Bears, which turned ugly and brutal in those days.

But the Packers were also tagged with off-field issues that, amazingly, saw two Packers, defensive back Mossy Cade and wide receiver James Lofton, in court on the same day on sexual assault charges.

It had gotten so bad, and on so many fronts, that in May 1987 the travails and decline of the Packers was chronicled in a detailed and rather scathing *Sports Illustrated* piece titled "Troubled Times in Titletown."

The story, by acclaimed *SI* writer Frank Deford, went into all the issues that were tearing away at the proud history of the franchise, including race, player accountability, and the very nature of an NFL franchise still in a place like Green Bay, Wisconsin. Tongue-in-cheek, he even suggested that the team buy itself from stockholders and set up shop in Milwaukee. But he also acknowledged the people of Green Bay would never let that happen.

He closed the story with this: "It has been almost two decades since Lombardi left the sidelines in Green Bay, and the Packers have only qualified for the playoffs twice during that time. They remain the team with the most championships in NFL history—11 titles for Titletown. But since Curly Lambeau, the team's founder, stepped down as Packer coach in 1949, only Lombardi has been able to forge a winning record for a career. Maybe the demographic deck is just too stacked against Green Bay. The scandals and defeats that have brought a sense of gloom and doom to the grand old franchise may seem even worse simply because, deep inside, the good people of Green Bay fear that this may be the way it's going to be from now on."

Only months later the NFL Players Association would go on strike, bringing on replacement players for three games and further alienating fans not only in Green Bay but around the league.

The Packers would finish with another dismal season, going 5–9–1, and its 12th sub-.500 season in the 20 years since Lombardi stepped down. After that season Gregg resigned to restart the scandal-plagued college program at his alma mater, Southern Methodist.

Then came another embarrassment for a franchise that thought it could sink no lower.

In an effort to find a new head coach who would not only turn around the Packers' fortunes on the field but also change the culture of defeatism permeating the facility, the Packers looked back to the college ranks and focused on George Perles, the no-nonsense veteran head coach who had worked wonders at Michigan State. Prior to that he had helped run the vaunted defense of the Pittsburgh Steelers before joining his alma mater in East Lansing in 1983.

After winning the Rose Bowl in 1987, the Packers believed Perles had agreed to leave MSU and join the Packers. So certain were they that a press release had already been written announcing Perles as head coach. But at the last minute, he changed his mind, claiming that "Spartan green runs in my veins."

Packers VP Tom Braatz, who coordinated the search, was dubious of that statement and believed Perles was pressured by Governor James Blanchard to stay at Michigan State with, of course, a substantial bump in his salary.

Two years later Perles was enticed to join the New York Jets as head coach, and the same scenario played out. Four years after that, with an NCAA investigation hanging over MSU's head, Perles was fired.

But the snub by a high-profile college coach was yet another black eye for a franchise that now wasn't sure just where the bottom of the barrel really was.

With Perles off the market, the Packers settled on Cleveland Browns offensive coordinator Lindy Infante, who jumped at the opportunity to become an NFL head coach. It would be another study in futility, however.

A terrible first season in 1988 (a 4–12 record, the second in three years for Green Bay) left no one with any reason to believe 1989 would be any better. But then a strange thing happened. For one magical season, everything that had gone wrong for so many years stopped going wrong—at least for the most part.

The ball bounced in the right direction. Players made plays. Situations that usually ended up disastrous suddenly did not. And for one remarkable season, the Packers were, more or less, relevant again.

Green Bay won 10 games in 1989, its best showing since 1972, with six of those wins by three points and three of those coming in the final seconds.

Dubbed the "Cardiac Pack" and led by a swashbuckling young quarterback named Don Majkowski, the Packers were fun to watch again. These Packers played with abandon and childlike enthusiasm, and they won by playing a brand of football that hadn't been seen in town in years.

But as well as they played, it wouldn't be enough to get Green Bay into the playoffs. That's because, despite a 10–6 record that tied the Minnesota Vikings for first place in the division, Green Bay lost out on tiebreakers to Minnesota, and in these days before multiple wild-card berths, the Packers stayed home.

But there was reason for hope and optimism and the belief that better days were ahead for the Packers. Fans were so pumped up, in fact, that in an off-season poll conducted by the *Milwaukee Sentinel*, fans voted Lindy Infante as the best coach in Packers history, edging out two guys named Lambeau and Lombardi.

The Packers had Majkowski, a rising star at quarterback, and they had a wide receiver in Sterling Sharpe who had the potential to develop into one of the game's top receivers. There was young, developing talent on defense, and, of course, they had the best coach in team history.

It all fell apart that following summer when Majkowski missed most of training camp in a contract holdout. By the time he returned to the team a week before the start of the season, the damage had been done and a potentially great campaign went off the rails before it had started. Green Bay reverted back to the team it had been for too long, going 6–10 followed by a 4–12 effort in 1991.

Packers President Bob Harlan could take no more. He had joined the franchise in 1971 as an assistant general manager and through the next two decades had a front-row seat for everything that had transpired.

Then in 1989, after rising through the ranks, he was named team president and it was time to make some franchise-shattering decisions—decisions that had to be made because the Packers' situation was not only untenable but, quite possibly, fatal for its future.

The Packers organization, as everyone who follows the team even a little knows, has no deep-pocketed multimillionaire owning the team. It is as it had ever been, a community-controlled, nonprofit organization in which thousands of fans own stock, a tradition that goes back to 1923 when, facing financial disaster, the team offered to sell stock for $3 a share to keep itself solvent.

The stockholders have no say in financial or personnel decisions and, really, the only tangible evidence of their ownership is a stock certificate that is often passed down through the generations.

The Packers stay viable through the staggeringly successful and lucrative TV deals negotiated by the NFL and which every team shares in. The Packers also make a lot of money from attendance, parking fees, merchandise sales, and all the other pieces that make every team viable.

It had been a long and successful partnership between the fans and the team, but by 1990 that relationship was starting to change. Two NFL work stoppages—in 1982 and again in 1987—had soured many fans, including in Green Bay where for decades it seemed nothing could damage that special bond.

But mediocre football over a long period of time, coupled with the recent strikes and off-field incidents, had led to the unthinkable: the Packers were no longer selling out Lambeau Field. Not only was that bad for prestige, it was bad for the team's bottom line.

Bob Harlan knew changes had to come or it was possible that the Packers could leave Green Bay—possibly headed to Milwaukee or just as possible, somewhere outside the state. As a disastrous 1991 season wound down, Harlan knew everything needed to be blown up and a fresh start made.

And his attention focused on Ron Wolf, a veteran of more than 20 seasons in the NFL as a personnel executive with four different teams. Blunt and decisive, Harlan was convinced Wolf would be the right fit for a directionless franchise.

Four years earlier Wolf had interviewed with Harlan for a similar position with the Packers, but the candidate told the president he was not interested. And there were no guarantees this time as Wolf, after being offered the GM position, talked with friends throughout the NFL about whether he should take it. All of them said no.

But Wolf, who at the time was director of player personnel for the New York Jets, believed there was untapped potential in Green Bay if the right people could be found to put it into action.

It was a new day and a new time, and Harlan would not take no for an answer this time. So he came back to Wolf with a staggering offer. As they sat in a Denny's restaurant in Green Bay, Harlan presented Wolf with an offer that left him stunned. He would be general manager of the Packers, but he'd also be much more than that. He'd be given the kind of unlimited power to make personnel decisions not seen in Green Bay since the days of Vince Lombardi.

"I was given complete personnel control," Wolf said. "My former mentor [Oakland Raiders owner/GM] Al Davis said it best when he told me it would be like you were an owner. It was control of the football side of the business and, my goodness, to have that opportunity to build your own legacy. What a great opportunity for a person to have. And especially with a franchise steeped in the tradition of the Packers. To have that opportunity to do that is what changed for me. It was hard to turn down."

So, in November 1991, Harlan announced Wolf as his new general manager, stating in a packed press conference quite simply and firmly, "He has total authority over every phase of the [football] operation and over every person in the player personnel area. What he does with the head coach, what he does with scouts, that's all his prerogative."

It was a remarkable and definitive statement about where the Packers had to go, and to put that kind of power in the hands of one man was a dramatic gamble. All these years later, Wolf still remembers the feeling.

"It's one of those things you can't believe the enormity of it," he said. "You're in the press conference and you realize you're the guy."

And Wolf wasted little time making clear what his future plans entailed.

"It's a dream come true," Wolf said at the press conference. "I consider it an honor to be joining an organization with the rich history and tradition of the Green Bay Packers. I want to assure Packer fans I will be doing everything in my power to make this football team a consistent contender and NFL champion once again."

To dubious and emotionally scarred Packers fans, it sounded good, but they had heard this all before. But something was different from the start. Wolf dove into the reimaging of the Packers—attending practices and games and putting a scouting staff together that would scour the college ranks and NFL to find players who would make a difference.

His first concrete realization, after watching practice and games, was that Infante had to be replaced. He had lost the respect of his players and Wolf could not abide that. The day after the 1991 season ended—ironically after the Packers played one of their best games of the season in a 27–7 win over the Minnesota Vikings—Wolf fired Infante and his entire staff.

The changes had begun, and they would continue rapidly over the next three years.

First, Wolf convinced and then signed Mike Holmgren, offensive coordinator of the San Francisco 49ers and the hottest NFL head-coaching prospect that year.

"I had been brought up believing defensive coaches made the best head coaches," Wolf said. "And I could point to guys like [the Dallas Cowboys'] Tom Landry and [the Pittsburgh Steelers'] Chuck Noll and [the Oakland Raiders'] John Madden and [the Miami Dolphins'] Don Shula. But suddenly it dawned on me that this thing had changed a little. Guys like [the San Francisco 49ers'] Bill Walsh and [the Washington Redskins'] Joe Gibbs and [Denver Broncos'] Dan Reeves were offensive guys. That's where the game was going, and that's when I began to look at the offensive side of the ball."

Initially, Wolf had hoped to lure former New York Giants head coach and close friend Bill Parcells to Green Bay. But Parcells was recovering from open-heart surgery and that would not be an option.

So his sights turned to Holmgren.

"No one had done more on the offensive side of the ball than Holmgren had in San Francisco," Wolf said. "A lot of teams wanted him. He was the girl with the curl."

Wolf's sales pitch to Holmgren was simple but dramatic.

"I told him we had a chance to resurrect a dead franchise," Wolf said. "And he was such a student of the game and he had such respect for the tradition of the Green Bay Packers, and I think that appealed to him. Fortunately, he cast his lot with the Packers."

Wolf then focused on finding a quarterback, but not just any quarterback. He wanted a young, confident, talented player that Holmgren could mold into the guy who could lead the Packers for years to come.

Wolf was certain that was Brett Favre, an untamed talent whom he had first seen in college and had never forgotten. Favre was languishing on the bench with the Atlanta Falcons, overweight and uninspired. Nicknamed the "Pillsbury Doughboy" by his head coach Jerry Glanville, the coach once told Favre the only way he'd see playing time was if every other quarterback died in a car wreck.

But Wolf knew better. He knew Favre's innate, almost unteachable, ability and he knew that in the right situation and with the right coaching and personnel, Favre could be a star.

So in a move that puzzled Packers fans and the NFL, Wolf offered Green Bay's first-round draft choice to the Falcons for Favre.

The Falcons were giddy at the thought of unloading Favre, who had taken up permanent residence in Glanville's doghouse. As well, Favre had a hip injury he suffered in a college all-star game that seemed further evidence the trade was a classic Packers misstep.

But Wolf saw greatness in Favre, and if he wouldn't last more than three seasons in the NFL before the injury would shut him down, as several doctors believed, Wolf was OK with that.

"We'll take whatever we can get from him," Wolf has related time and again.

It turned out to be substantially more than three seasons.

But now comes the first key game in Favre's Packers career— perhaps not one of the most important but certainly one that resides in the neighborhood. And it set the tone for so much more to come.

It was now the 1992 season, the first for Holmgren, Favre, and Wolf in their new environment, and it had gotten off to a miserable start.

A season-opening home overtime loss to the Minnesota Vikings had been followed up by a train wreck in Tampa as Green Bay committed three turnovers, managed barely 200 yards of offense, and were flattened by the Buccaneers, 31–3.

Starting quarterback Don Majkowski had been ineffective, and Favre got his first game action as a Packer late in the contest. And as every Packers fan now knows, his first completion was a batted ball caught by . . . Favre himself.

Now the Packers came home winless to face the 2–0 Cincinnati Bengals, and Holmgren, only half-jokingly, told the media that he might be the first NFL coach fired after never winning a game.

But when Bengals nose tackle Tim Krumrie fell on Majkowski's ankle in the first quarter, forcing him from the game and sending in Favre, the axis of the Earth changed and the Green Bay Packers would never be the same.

What happened after that is now part of Packers legend and lore.

The stories, of course, have taken on lives of their own in the intervening years as Favre was reputed to have called plays and formations that never even existed. But this much is true: to everyone who watched the game—from the sun-splashed Lambeau Field crowd to the media to those who watched on TV and to curious onlookers around the NFL—a lightning bolt had surged through the Packers and everything with the franchise and the perception of it would change.

Sacked five times and nearly throwing three interceptions, Favre led a frantic fourth-quarter rally that saw him throw his first NFL touchdown pass, a five-yarder to Sterling Sharpe. Then, in the play burned into every Packers fan's brain, came the perfect 35-yard scoring toss to

Kitrick Taylor, with 13 seconds remaining, to win the game. After the play Favre ripped off his helmet and celebrated like a little kid. It would be a scene repeated a thousand times in stadiums around the NFL.

Favre completed 22 of 39 passes for 289 yards and no interceptions. But more to the point, he injected a life into the Packers that had not been seen in years.

"Tough kid," veteran center James Campen said after the game. "He's like an offensive lineman playing quarterback."

Truth be told, even if Majkowski had not been injured, Holmgren might well have replaced him with Favre sometime in the game. And if Majkowski's damaged ankle had somehow magically healed by the following week, Favre would still have started. It was predestined.

That Bengals game was the first step. The next week, in another home game against the Pittsburgh Steelers, would be the second.

Pro football is littered with examples of unknown players coming into a game and doing remarkable things. But often, by the next week, rivals have studied that unknown player to the point where he's not unknown any longer and he comes crashing to the ground.

But Favre showed against the always tough Steelers that he would not be a one-game wonder. He played controlled, smart football, completing 14 of 19 passes with two more touchdowns and, again, no interceptions, and led the Packers to a 17–3 victory.

The job was his.

Of course, it would not be golden all season for the Packers or Favre. Green Bay lost four of its next five games, followed by a six-game winning streak and, with a chance to somehow gain a playoff spot in the season finale, Favre threw three interceptions in a dismal effort against the Vikings.

But the point had been made. The Packers had found their quarterback to take them forward, and Ron Wolf continued to put the pieces in place to ensure that upward trajectory would continue.

In fact, one of those pieces helped beat up Brett Favre during a 27–24 Packers win at Milwaukee County Stadium in the 1992 season.

The league's most dominant defensive player, Philadelphia's Reggie White, was growing restless and frustrated with the Eagles, a talented team in the regular season that just couldn't seem to put it together when the playoffs rolled around.

In 1992 White was in his final contract season with Philadelphia and had no plans to re-sign with the Eagles. That meant an off-season free-agency frenzy, which was just getting started in the NFL back then.

Simply, White wanted to play for a team that had made the commitment to reach the Super Bowl, a commitment he didn't believe the Eagles would, or could, make.

But on this November afternoon in Milwaukee, White wasn't thinking about contracts. He was thinking about separating the Packers' new young quarterback from his senses. White battered Favre several times during the game, even driving him to the ground and injuring Favre's shoulder.

But Favre popped up after that hit, slapped White on the helmet and said, "Great hit, Reg."

"I didn't even really know who he was," White said after the game. "But I was really impressed with how he played the game. Tough, competitive, he really loves playing."

Favre shook off his sore shoulder and two interceptions and threw for 275 yards and two touchdowns as the Packers beat the play-off-bound Eagles that day (and who again fell short in the postseason).

The off-season free-agency frenzy did indeed follow for White, and after dismissing offers from two of the league's powerhouses— Washington and San Francisco—White stunned the NFL, and Packers fans everywhere, by signing with Green Bay.

The four-year, $17 million deal was certainly a driving force in White's decision, but he also admitted that Brett Favre was the kind of quarterback who could lead a team to a championship, and he wanted to be a part of that.

The Packers finished 9–7 in 1992, barely missing the playoffs. But unlike the 10–6 record of three years earlier, this record was built on a young, solid foundation. It did not require a host of last-second wins and it didn't require more luck than skill. This was a team being built for the long haul, and while 1992 was the first glimpse of that, it was the 1993 season where it came together.

Which brings us to our next most important game in franchise history. Again, this one may be up for dispute and argument, but facts are facts. In 1993 Green Bay posted the same 9–7 record it did in 1992, but this time it was good enough to earn a spot in the playoffs as the wild-card team.

Green Bay's first trip to the playoffs since 1982 was viewed by many as just another aberration, a team that caught enough luck to slip in. Perhaps.

Indeed, after securing their playoff spot with a win over the Los Angeles Raiders the week before, the Packers traveled to the Silverdome in Pontiac, Michigan, and were terrible. Favre threw for just 190 yards and was intercepted four times, giving him a league-high 24 picks that season. The Packers lost, 30–20, and as their consolation for the wild-card berth, they would get to return to the Silverdome the following week to play the division champions again.

But this is where Favre was different from so many others. In the third quarter of a tight game, Lions cornerback Melvin Jenkins intercepted Favre and returned it 15 yards for a touchdown and a 17–7 Detroit lead. It was a play that could have wrecked the confidence of many quarterbacks, but Favre simply brought the Packers back on a 72-yard drive that ended in a touchdown pass to Sterling Sharpe.

It was a back-and-forth effort from there by both teams—with the Lions relying on their star running back Barry Sanders (169 yards rushing) and the Packers countering with Favre (204 passing yards, three touchdowns).

Then with two minutes and 26 seconds remaining in the game and trailing 24–21, the Packers had one more opportunity. Favre drove his team to the Lions' 40 and on second down, after being forced from the pocket and to his left, he launched a rocket across the field to a wide-open Sterling Sharpe in the end zone.

The Packers' coaching staff had been hoping simply to get the ball close enough for a game-tying field goal and overtime. But when Favre saw Sharpe streaking down the right sideline, he took advantage.

"Great presence of mind on Brett's part," Packers quarterback coach Steve Mariucci told the *Milwaukee Journal*.

"It was the play of the year," coach Mike Holmgren said in the press conference afterward. "It's just a wonderful, wonderful feeling. We worked so hard to get this one."

"This is a big monkey off our backs," Ron Wolf said.

Wolf also points to that victory as one of the most important certainly in his tenure with the Packers.

"There was no way we were supposed to win that game," Wolf said recently. "I remember listening later to the radio replay of that game with Jack Buck and Hank Stram and they kept saying, 'Detroit's going to win, Detroit's got this.' But they didn't. I'll tell you one of the most amazing players I've ever been around was Sterling Sharpe. If one guy deserves to be in the Pro Football Hall of Fame, it's him. At the end of that game, the Lions left him alone. How do they do that?"

The victory proved two things: First, the Packers had been outplayed on the road but had found a way to rally and win the kind of game they could not have won even the year before.

"All indications were that we were going to lose that game," Wolf recalled. "And it was certainly a key game because it was a playoff game."

The second? That this kid Favre could play.

"He's a very talented young man," Holmgren said.

The Packers would go to Dallas the following week to play the defending Super Bowl champion Cowboys, who had blasted the Packers earlier in the season, 36–14. And while this game was closer, there was never a real sense the Packers were on the Cowboys' level—at least not yet.

Favre threw for 331 yards and two touchdowns but the Packers knew what they still had to do, and as they looked across the field to the Cowboys sideline, they saw what they wanted to be when they grew up.

The Cowboys would go on to win their second straight Super Bowl three weeks later, but the Packers had learned some valuable and unforgettable lessons.

And even in the ever-evolving world of the NFL, the Packers knew time was on their side.

"HEY, MAYBE GREEN BAY IS FOR REAL"

PACKERS 27, SAN FRANCISCO 49ERS 17

JANUARY 6, 1996

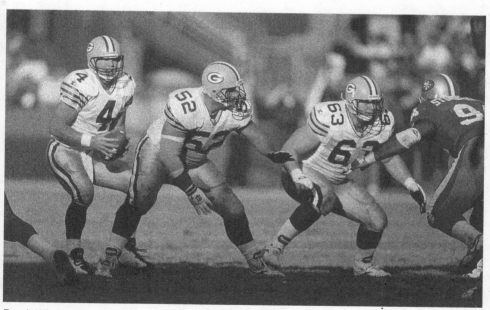

Frank Winters (52) and Adam Timmerman (63) block for Brett Favre during the 1996 NFC Divisional Playoff game against the 49ers. PAUL SPINELLI VIA AP

CHAPTER EIGHT

"HEY, MAYBE GREEN BAY IS FOR REAL"

PACKERS 27, SAN FRANCISCO 49ERS 17

JANUARY 6, 1996

Frank Winters (52) and Adam Timmerman (63) block for Brett Favre during the 1995 NFC Divisional Playoff game against the 49ers.

THERE IS ALWAYS THE BELIEF THAT YOU ARE GOOD ENOUGH TO COMpete with the best. But belief without proof is nothing more than shouting at the rain.

So it was for the Green Bay Packers of the mid-1990s. The duo of general manager Ron Wolf and head coach Mike Holmgren had slowly and methodically rebuilt the Packers from NFL afterthoughts to an interesting, if incomplete, story.

It was only five years earlier when the Packers were a joke. A franchise in the middle of nowhere going, not coincidentally, nowhere. Attendance was sliding and revenues were falling and for many NFL players, the thought of playing in Green Bay was only a step away from being waived altogether.

But team president Bob Harlan moved aggressively, hired Wolf as general manager, and gave him carte blanche to remake this team as he felt was necessary. He hired Holmgren as his head coach, traded for the potential-laden but still unknown Brett Favre as his quarterback, and stunned pro football by putting together a financial package to lure the game's top free agent, defensive end Reggie White.

But those were the moves everyone knows about and celebrates. There were so many other smaller, behind-the-headlines moves that were just as significant.

For example, Wolf's first draft as Packers general manager in 1992 uncovered three key starters who would make huge contributions over the next few seasons: wide receiver Robert Brooks (third round), running back Edgar Bennett (fourth round), and tight end Mark Chmura (sixth round).

Wolf did it again in 1993 when four eventual starters were picked: linebacker Wayne Simmons and cornerback George Teague in the first round, offensive tackle Earl Dotson in the third round, and cornerback Doug Evans in the sixth round. As well, two key reserves were taken that year in linebacker James Willis and defensive tackle Bob Kuberski.

The restructuring continued in the 1994 draft with guard Aaron Taylor in the first round (though his career was cut short by numerous knee injuries), defensive tackle Gabe Wilkins in the fourth round, running back Dorsey Levens in the fifth, and wide receiver Bill Schroeder in the sixth.

Then in 1995 Wolf showed his real genius as 5 of his 10 draft picks ended up starting almost immediately: cornerback Craig Newsome (first round); all three third-round picks in fullback William Henderson, linebacker Brian Williams, and wide receiver Antonio Freeman; and guard Adam Timmerman (seventh round).

Those draft picks, along with key free-agent signings such as wide receiver Mark Ingram, defensive end Sean Jones, and linebacker Fred Strickland, as well as key pieces already in place such as center Frank Winters, linebacker Bryce Paup, and safety LeRoy Butler, had turned the Packers into more than a novelty.

"We had a pretty good team by then," Wolf recalled. "We just had to prove it."

And the 1995 season would provide that opportunity. But first, these young Packers still needed another lesson on how to win when it mattered most.

In 1993 everything was new to these Packers. They posted a 9–7 record, reached the playoffs for the first time in 10 years, and, frankly, were happy to be there. A stunning first-round playoff win on the road in Detroit was a bonus before they were summarily dismissed in the next round by the powerhouse Dallas Cowboys. It was a lesson learned.

In 1994 the Packers again posted a 9–7 regular-season mark, reaching the playoffs in dramatic fashion in the next-to-last game and, after 62 years, the final game to be played by the Packers in Milwaukee.

In that game Favre rallied the Packers 67 yards in the final minutes against the Atlanta Falcons, rolling right, running nine yards, and diving into the end zone with 14 seconds to play. It secured a 21–17 victory and a spot in the playoffs.

Their reward as a wild card was to again play the Detroit Lions, their division rival with whom they had split two games during the regular season. But the Lions, also a wild card that season, were still seething from that playoff loss to Green Bay the previous season, a game in which they believed they had dominated and should have won.

But this was a different Packers team as well. More mature, more focused, and emboldened by the fact that the game would be played at Lambeau Field, the Packers knew the way to victory was to shut down the longtime pain in their backsides, the Lions' incredible running back Barry Sanders.

On artificial turf, Sanders was nearly unstoppable. On slick grass and frozen turf in Green Bay? Not so much.

Green Bay's crafty and veteran defensive coordinator Fritz Shurmur also had a plan that he demanded his defense stick to. He wanted every defensive lineman to maintain the same space at the point of attack on every play to eliminate Sanders's ability to cut back on runs.

"Like the tines of a fork," Shurmur said.

It worked. Sanders, who had gashed the Packers for 169 yards on the ground the previous year in the playoffs and only a month earlier had piled up another 188 yards rushing on Green Bay, managed minus-1 yard on 13 carries, and the Lions were held to a playoff-record low minus-4 total rushing yards in Green Bay's solid 16–12 victory.

The next step was another trip to Dallas to face the defending Super Bowl champion Cowboys, who were on a mission to win three straight titles—something that hadn't been done since the Packers of the mid-1960s did it.

Yet again, the Cowboys made quick work of the Packers at Texas Stadium as quarterback Troy Aikman completed passes almost at will on the way to 337 yards passing and two touchdowns, including a 94-yard TD bomb to Alvin Harper. The Cowboys won again, 35–9, and just like the year before, they had barely broken a sweat doing so.

By that stage the Packers had lost five straight to the Cowboys, and few of them had been especially close. It had been one of the great rivalries of the 1960s, but now Dallas had shown they had taken command. In fact, during the 1990s the Packers and Cowboys played 10 times and Dallas won nine of those matchups.

Yet, as had been the case in 1993, the Packers did take away some more valuable, if excruciating, lessons that they believed would benefit them the next year.

And in 1995 the Packers had grown up. In his first three seasons as head coach, Holmgren had fashioned three 9–7 records and two playoff berths. And while those results were certainly preferable to the rampant mediocrity of a decade earlier, it was time to move forward. And they did.

A surprising season-opening home loss to the Los Angeles Rams would be followed by Green Bay winning five of six and then closing the season by winning six of seven, including the season finale at home, where the name Yancey Thigpen even now will always bring a smile to the faces of Packers fans.

The Packers knew a victory in their finale against the Pittsburgh Steelers would sew up the NFC Central Division title, Green Bay's first full-season title since 1972.

In a rugged and entertaining back-and-forth game on Christmas Eve in which Favre was hit so hard he was spitting up blood, the Steelers, who had already wrapped up the AFC Central title, were driving toward a game-winning touchdown in the final seconds. But when quarterback Neil O'Donnell saw Thigpen wide-open in the end zone and tossed him the ball, the All-Pro wide receiver simply dropped it.

The Packers escaped with the 24–19 win, and as they celebrated their division title in one locker room, Thigpen could only smile in the other locker room.

"Merry Christmas, Packers fans," he said.

The Packers finished that season 11–5, their highest win total since they went 12–2 in 1966—and yes the 1995 Packers played two more games. But the point was made. The Packers were on the doorstep of something special.

Brett Favre had a remarkable season, completing 63 percent of his passes for a league-best 4,413 yards and 38 touchdowns, also a league best. He was named MVP for his efforts, the first of three he would win as a Packer.

Robert Brooks replaced the retired Sterling Sharpe and caught 99 passes for 1,497 yards and 13 scores.

On defense, Reggie White posted 12 sacks and Sean Jones nine, and safety LeRoy Butler was becoming a force as well, intercepting five passes and leading the team in tackles.

It was now clear that reaching the playoffs was no longer enough, and with these new and rather daunting expectations, the Packers would get their first chance to prove it when they hosted the Atlanta Falcons in the opening round.

The Falcons presented an interesting challenge for the Packers in the person of quarterback Jeff George, who had played almost as well as Favre during the season, throwing for more than 4,100 yards and 24 touchdowns. And George had three superb wide receivers—Eric Metcalf (108 catches, eight touchdowns), Terance Mathis (74 catches, nine touchdowns), and Bert Emanuel (74 catches, five touchdowns). All three had posted more than 1,000 yards in receptions, something not even the high-powered Packers offense could claim.

Not surprisingly, the Falcons wasted little time demonstrating what was to come as, on their first possession, George hit Metcalf for a 65-yard scoring pass.

But again, this was a new, mature Packers team, and an early quick strike like that was nothing to be concerned about. Two Favre touchdown passes and a 76-yard punt return for a touchdown by Antonio Freeman staked the Packers to a 27–10 halftime lead, and they would cruise from there, beating Atlanta 37–20.

While George threw for 366 yards and two scores on 54 attempts, he was also intercepted twice as Atlanta abandoned its running game. Meanwhile, Favre was coolly efficient, throwing for 199 yards and two scores while Edgar Bennett put up Jim Taylor–type numbers with 24 carries, 108 yards, and a touchdown.

For the third straight year, the Packers had won their first-round playoff game and this was where the wheels usually fell off. Many NFL observers felt that would happen again as the Packers had to travel to San Francisco to face the defending Super Bowl champion 49ers.

Everything seemed stacked against Green Bay. They would travel halfway across the country to play a team brimming with confidence. They featured the top offense in the NFL and the no. 2 defense, and their quarterback, the dangerous Steve Young, was healthy again and ready for the challenge. On top of that, as the NFC's top seed, they had the previous week off and were rested.

Oddsmakers made the 49ers 10-point favorites, a staggering number for a second-round playoff game between two supposedly evenly matched teams. But at that point, no one yet believed in the Packers—except the Packers themselves.

In the end it may have been one of the finest, most complete performances ever by a Packers team in a game that meant so much.

Carrying a chip on their shoulders the size of Montana, the Packers strode into 3Com Park and simply overwhelmed the champs before they knew what hit them. It was a game that was especially important to Holmgren, the Bay Area native who had hoped to one day coach the team that meant so much to him.

Holmgren had played football at Lincoln High before moving on to play college ball as a quarterback at the University of Southern California.

He then moved back to the Bay Area, where he began his coaching career at San Francisco State before coaching and teaching at the high school level, first at his alma mater Lincoln High and then at Sacred Heart Cathedral Prep, where he lived so meagerly he once cracked, "The nuns paid us in wine."

But he was on the fast track as a football coach and next went to Oak Grove High in nearby San Jose, where his teams thrived. Next it was on to the college ranks, where he was quarterbacks coach for the offensive powerhouses at Brigham Young.

By that stage Holmgren was already earning a reputation as a coach who knew how to get the best from quarterbacks—including one at BYU named Steve Young.

And when an opening for a quarterbacks coach opened with the 49ers in 1986, head coach Bill Walsh looked to Holmgren to help tutor his already-legendary quarterback Joe Montana and, eventually, Young.

Three years later Holmgren was the 49ers' offensive coordinator under new head coach George Seifert, and his name was at or near the top of every NFL team's list when it came to head-coaching candidates.

As the 1991 season wound down, and teams in need began searching for a coaching replacement for the following season, everyone knew about Holmgren. Indeed, six NFL teams, including the Packers, contacted Holmgren about his interest in their club and, depending on the sources you'd like to believe, he seriously considered four.

But it was the Packers that intrigued him most. And even though he had recently signed a new contract with the 49ers, a deal was worked out that would send Green Bay's second-round draft pick in 1992 to San Francisco to pry Holmgren loose.

"This is where I want to be," Holmgren said in that January 1992 press conference announcing his hiring. "The Packers are set up to succeed. It's important to turn it around and we will do that."

Then he added: "We'll talk about a timetable a little later."

Now, four seasons later, the time had come and he was facing a team he respected and loved in a place where the roots still ran deep (in fact, he owned a home in nearby Santa Cruz and had written into his first Packers contract that if the 49ers head-coaching job became available, he would be allowed to leave to pursue it).

But none of that mattered right now. The 49ers, who had routed the San Diego Chargers in the last Super Bowl and were expected to return again this year, were the kind of team the Packers had to beat to be taken seriously as an NFL contender.

And with 7:31 left to play in the first quarter, the Packers made their first statement that they, indeed, needed to be taken seriously.

49ers quarterback Steve Young threw a swing pass to running back Adam Walker, who was almost immediately hit by linebacker Wayne Simmons. Walker fumbled and cornerback Craig Newsome was there to scoop it up and run 31 yards for the touchdown.

"I remember the game Wayne Simmons had that day," Wolf recalled recently. "He was such a dominant performer in that game. Great player."

The quick strike stunned the 49ers and the sellout crowd at 3Com Park, which was expecting a quick walkover against the pretenders. But it also ignited the Packers and reinforced what they had believed all along: that they could play with anyone.

As well, Brett Favre was magnificent. He threw strike after strike against the confused Niners defense. Following Newsome's score, Favre directed the Packers offense on two more scoring drives that resulted in touchdown passes to tight end Keith Jackson and, early in the second quarter, to fellow tight end Mark Chmura.

Barely into the second quarter, the Packers held a 21–0 lead that would not be challenged.

The Packers defense swarmed Young, sacking him four times and intercepting two passes. And while Jerry Rice, San Francisco's incomparable wide receiver, caught 11 passes, he did not reach the end zone.

"One of the great statements that I've ever been around was when Mike Holmgren told [defensive coordinator] Fritz Shurmur, 'I don't care what else you do, don't let Jerry Rice beat us,'" Wolf said recently. "And he never really did."

In the end the Packers rang up 368 yards on offense and Favre cemented his reputation as the NFL's new gunslinger, completing 21 of 29 passes for 299 yards and two touchdowns.

In the jubilant Packers' locker room afterward, players spoke in ways that had not been heard in a Packers locker room in years.

"I think people are going to be saying, 'Hey, maybe Green Bay is for real,'" Favre said at the press conference.

Said linebacker George Koonce to the *Milwaukee Journal*: "I think the 49ers took us for granted."

This was especially sweet for defensive end Reggie White, the game's top pass rusher, who had taken the risk (and the big free-agent contract) by joining the Packers three years earlier in the belief that this was the team to finally get him to a Super Bowl.

"This is really sweet," he said. "This is the farthest I've ever gotten."

Coach Mike Holmgren smiled afterward and said simply, "I think we can go all the way. Why not?"

Well, there was still one massive "why not?" facing the Packers, and it was a familiar one.

By eliminating the 49ers, the Packers had clearly made a statement that a changing of the guard in the NFC was commencing. But until they got by the Dallas Cowboys, who now waited for them in the NFC Championship Game, it would be an incomplete journey.

Wolf saw the significance of that win as well.

"The thing was to establish yourself in the NFC, and to do that you had to beat the people on top," he said recently. "And the people on top were the San Francisco 49ers. What I hold dearly is the fact that in the time I was there we only lost to the 49ers once, and I think that's a great tribute to the players."

And as the 49ers, almost to a man, commended the Packers for their performance at 3Com, they also all said that, at least for now, the Cowboys were simply better.

Now, for the third straight year, Green Bay would travel to Dallas to meet the Cowboys in the playoffs. The first two trips had gone badly— a 27–17 loss in January 1994 and a 35–9 walkover 12 months later.

Now, the Packers were convinced they were better, more mature, and more experienced than at the previous two meetings. But until they won, it would just be so much talk.

And it was a better performance. The Packers hit the Cowboys in the mouth more than a few times, as a blocked punt and a strong offensive performance saw Green Bay take a 27–24 lead into the fourth quarter.

But in the end, the Cowboys again were simply too much. Emmitt Smith rushed for 150 yards and three touchdowns and the Cowboys defense intercepted Favre twice, turning both into eventual touchdowns. It was simply too much to overcome.

It was a loss that hurt more than probably most Packers felt it would. It wasn't as though they didn't realize the power and talent and maturity of the Cowboys, a team that had taken them to school each of the last three years. But this one really stung because of the way Green Bay had played the week before in San Francisco and to realize that, needing just one more great quarter of football against Dallas, they couldn't close the deal.

"We fell apart," defensive end Sean Jones said in disgust.

Yes, they had, and those mistakes were costly and avoidable. And, as usual, the Cowboys made them pay.

"We keep coming down and getting lessons," a visibly frustrated Mike Holmgren said after the game. "I'm tired of getting lessons."

But as much as the loss hurt, in some ways it also proved to be different from all the others. And it would call to mind the Willie Davis story from 1960 after the Packers, then also a young and developing team, had lost the championship to the Philadelphia Eagles.

After that game, Vince Lombardi had stood up and told his disconsolate team that, as long as he was head coach, this would be the last time the Packers would lose a championship game. And it was, as Green Bay would go on to reach five title games in the next seven years and win them all.

Now, as the Packers flew home from Dallas after another defeat, Holmgren walked the aisle of the plane telling his team, "Remember how this feels. Don't ever forget it."

Star safety LeRoy Butler remembers.

"He told us, 'We didn't get it done this time, but we're going to get there. We all vowed to come back in the best shape of our lives and do whatever it took to get back. That's all we thought about."

So the seeds were planted that January night for a season that was still seven months away. Indeed, several Packers would admit in training camp before the 1996 season began that Holmgren's pep talk had become their rallying cry. Of course, Holmgren really didn't have to say anything because the players, almost to a man, knew what was needed, what was expected, what was demanded.

This was the team Ron Wolf envisioned when he took the job as general manager in the wreckage of the 1991 season. The coach he had hired, the players he had brought in through free agency and the draft, the quarterback no one knew about in 1992 but was now one of the best and most exciting players in the NFL had come together.

They had, as Holmgren had remarked after the latest loss to the Cowboys, learned another hard lesson, and now this team—mature, talented, driven, and smart—was ready to take that final step toward bringing the Green Bay Packers back among the ranks of the NFL elite.

What could stop them? How about a stunning off-season phone call from Brett Favre to Mike Holmgren that threatened to derail a career, much less a season?

CHAPTER NINE

"BACK WHERE IT BELONGS"

PACKERS 35, NEW ENGLAND PATRIOTS 21

JANUARY 26, 1997

Reggie White celebrates after sacking Drew Bledsoe in Super Bowl XXXI. AP PHOTO/KEVIN TERRELL

RON WOLF STOOD BEHIND THE NORTH END ZONE AT LAMBEAU FIELD, tears welling in his eyes. The noise from the raucous Lambeau Field crowd was reverberating around the ancient bowl of the stadium. Despite below-zero temperatures, every seat was, again, occupied, but few in attendance were sitting.

The final seconds of the NFC Championship Game were ticking down and the Packers, leading 30–13 over the game but overmatched Carolina Panthers, were awash in celebration.

Reggie White, his eyes ablaze, found Brett Favre and wrapped his arms around him.

"We did it," White said to Favre. "You're the reason I came here and we did it."

Favre shouted to White, "This is for you, Reg."

And there was Ron Wolf, the architect of the new NFC champs standing there watching like a proud father, soaking in an atmosphere unlike anything he had ever experienced before.

Asked if this was better than he expected, he said simply, "Damn right it is."

Recently, he spoke again about how important that victory was.

"Without a doubt, it was the best moment of my life in professional football because everyone said it couldn't happen in Green Bay," he said. "And lo and behold, it happened. That moment we won the NFC title against Carolina I am still unable to describe my feelings because of what it meant to me personally. It was the proudest moment of my entire 38 years in pro football. It was bigger than winning the Super Bowl."

And with that victory over the Panthers, who had upset the Dallas Cowboys the week before and denied the Packers a chance at some major postseason revenge, Green Bay was headed back to the Super Bowl for the first time in 30 years.

So much had transpired in those 30 years for the franchise that it made the head spin. From Lombardi's retirement to his resignation to his death, all in a matter of three years, the Packers had absorbed so much.

Great players had come and gone. Of course, bad coaches had, too. Fans had watched as their proud organization had fallen into disrepair and dysfunction to the point where younger fans had never known anything but mediocre football.

The NFL had changed and grown and become a corporate behemoth, and Green Bay seemed to have been left behind. The Packers no longer played games in Milwaukee, and there was serious talk of renovating Lambeau Field and, amazingly, even trying to build a larger stadium outside Green Bay. There had been some great wins but more heartbreaking losses and, over the years, it was becoming evident that, just maybe, the Packers could no longer compete.

But then a new regime came in and made substantial and necessary changes, and for four years these new Packers had teased fans, stepping up to the edge of greatness only to take another step back.

But on this day, as the sun started to sink and the temperature dropped at Lambeau Field, no one remembered any of that. The Pack was back and now they would set their sights on Super Bowl XXXI in New Orleans two weeks hence. They would face the AFC champion New England Patriots, but for many players the real goal had already been met. They were back in the Super Bowl and that meant everything.

Then again, it was only eight months earlier that a team built first to compete and then for greatness, and with the determination every player had to reach that goal, there were real questions whether it would, or could, happen.

That's because there were real questions as to the future of the most integral part of the Packers' equation: Brett Favre.

Since taking over the starting role early in the 1992 season, Favre had started every game. And in almost every one of those games, the ultra-competitive Favre took a beating. Yes, he was also commended for a childlike love of football, but that enthusiasm often led him to take risks that made his coach, his teammates, and fans cringe.

He was a player who was nothing close to fragile but for whom injury seemed to follow. In college at Southern Mississippi, Favre was involved in a car wreck two months before the start of his senior season that left him with a concussion and required the surgical removal of 30 inches of his intestines.

Yet, still recovering from the injuries that left him weak and underweight, he went out on the field and helped engineer an upset win over Alabama. Ron Wolf, then a scout for the Los Angeles Raiders, saw that game and was instantly transfixed.

There would be more. In 1995 and on his way to his first league MVP, Favre was battered and beaten up all season but never flinched.

In a midseason loss to the Minnesota Vikings, Favre suffered a severely sprained ankle that did force him out of the game.

During the week that followed, as the Packers prepared for their ancient rivals the Chicago Bears, it seemed clear Favre would not be able to play. The ankle was an interesting shade of green and yellow and was still severely swollen, and Holmgren, convinced his star quarterback wouldn't be able to walk much less avoid a Bears pass rush, signed a journeyman who knew Holmgren's system well, Bob Gagliano, to step in and play.

But the grit and determination and, yes, stubbornness, of Brett Favre was again on display. He was going to play, he told Holmgren. He didn't know how, but he would.

So that Sunday, cold and overcast with a hint of snow in the air and with his ankle taped so heavily it looked like a cast, Favre played—and played superbly. Barely able to walk much less maneuver in the pocket, Favre had one of his best games as a Packer. He completed 25 of 33 passes for 336 yards and five touchdowns with no interceptions as Green Bay prevailed, 35–28.

"I don't know what to say about that," Holmgren said. "Unbelievable."

But there was more. In the season finale against the Pittsburgh Steelers, Favre was scrambling for yardage when he was clobbered by Steelers linebacker Kevin Greene. Dazed and doubled over, Favre spit up blood but refused to leave the game.

In the end, his numbers were again impressive—23 of 31 for 301 yards and two touchdowns—as Green Bay secured the division title.

But those were just the injuries made public. Few, if anyone, knew of the beatings he took in every game and how, the morning after a game, there were times he simply could not get out of bed because he was in so much pain.

So, as early as the 1992 season, he began taking the powerful pain-killer Vicodin. First, he took the dose recommended by doctors until the time those doses no longer seemed to work. That's when pain relief began to morph into addiction.

In the 1997 book *Favre: For the Record*, which he cowrote with *Green Bay Press-Gazette* columnist Chris Havel, Favre recounted just how bad it had gotten.

He said his addiction to Vicodin had begun late in the 1994 season and he had to battle health issues from constipation to dehydration. He had other problems, too.

"The biggest problem wasn't getting the pills down, it was keeping them down," Favre wrote. "Most of the time, I'd just throw them right back up and they'd land on the floor. No big deal. I'd just pick the pills out of the vomit, rinse them off and try again."

In a 2016 *In Depth with Graham Bensinger* interview, Favre revealed more details, hidden for years, of a long-term and dramatic addiction.

"I tell people all the time that I took 15 Vicodin ES at one time. And they're like, 'It didn't knock you out?' It did totally the opposite—I was up. And that's kind of the way with addictions, too. What it's supposed to do, it doesn't," Favre said. "So when you take two pain pills, you're knocked out and you don't feel pain and you wake up, what, four, five, six hours later. I would be up just talking, I didn't want to sleep. Until about 10 o'clock the next morning when we were in offensive meetings was about the only time I wanted to sleep. Not a good time to sleep! And I would doze off, leaning back into a coat rack in our quarterback's meeting room.

"This went on for a long time. It wasn't just '96. That's when people knew about it because of the announcement. I don't know, it started three years before? I was taking pain pills before that but maybe not abusing them."

The announcement Favre referred to came in May of 1996 and reverberated through the NFL like an earthquake.

In a hastily arranged press conference and with Holmgren by his side, Favre announced he would be admitting himself to a drug treatment center for his addiction to painkillers.

The impetus for the decision? He had recently suffered a seizure in a Green Bay hospital that had been viewed by his eight-year-old daughter, Brittany, who asked her mother if Daddy was going to die.

So he quit cold turkey and sought help.

While obviously a smart and noble decision, thoughts that summer turned to just what would happen to the Green Bay Packers and a season that seemed so bright with optimism and potential. Could Favre be the same quarterback he had been?

Sure, there were always other questions that every NFL team had to answer as a new season approached. But for the Packers, whose expectations were so high, one question loomed. And whether it was fair or not, that question revolved around Favre and how he would respond to his tribulations.

He spent 46 turbulent days in the Menninger Clinic in Topeka, Kansas, battling doctors and staff as well as his demons and attempting to get clean with the goal of returning to the one place where everything made sense—the football field.

In a press conference prior to the start of training camp, Favre said all the right things, but one phrase stood out when the questions about his future continued unabated.

He smiled and said simply, "Bet against me. You'll lose."

In the season opener, Favre would get his first test and it would be a tough one: playing the always physical Tampa Bay Buccaneers in early September in Tampa. No bargain.

But something happened before the game even started that provided fans a glimpse of just where the quarterback was in his headspace. A thundershower swept over Tampa, and as Favre stood on the field during warmups, he smiled, opened his mouth, and let the rain in.

It was his inner child once again making an appearance and proving that, as he had always said, he had not changed and that football was, in the final essence, just a game played by kids.

He then proceeded to dismantle the Bucs. He threw three first-half touchdowns on the way to completing 20 of 27 passes for 247 yards and four scores.

After the resounding 34–3 victory, he stood before the relentlessly dubious media.

"There were questions about me?" Favre cracked. "I think that question's been answered. I told you guys a long time ago to bet against me. I don't know where your money is, but . . ."

For his teammates, if there was any doubt before, that game had erased it.

"Same old Brett," said tight end and close friend Mark Chmura.

"I would have been more surprised if he didn't play well," Holmgren said.

It would be the start of a season to remember for the Packers as Favre, spurred by the doubters and critics, unleashed another MVP season. He would throw for 3,899 yards and 39 touchdowns. More impressive was that he threw just 13 interceptions, matching his career-low with Green Bay, which he set the year before. But this season, every opponent knew who the key player was on offense, and rival defenses tried everything to slow him down.

Instead, the Packers rung up the NFL's best offense as well as the best defense, which allowed a then NFL-record low 210 points.

This was the team Ron Wolf had envisioned in his most vivid imagination only a few years earlier.

There were no weaknesses anywhere, even on special teams, where Green Bay featured a weapon they had never anticipated in the preseason: Desmond Howard.

The former Heisman Trophy winner and first-round draft pick of the Washington Redskins had seen his pro career sputter after three nondescript seasons in Washington and another with the Jacksonville Jaguars.

In 1996 the Packers were seeking a boost to their offense as well as the special teams and decided to give Howard a look, signing him as a free agent.

But in the preseason, a crucial time for Howard to show the coaching staff what he could do, he showed nothing. A hip injury not only kept him from playing in the first two preseason games, it kept him from practicing at all.

"If we'd only played two preseason games, he wouldn't have made the team," Holmgren said.

Fortunately for Howard and the Packers, the preseason went a little longer, and in the finale, a home game against the Pittsburgh Steelers, a still-gimpy Howard, knowing he needed to prove himself, returned a punt 77 yards for a touchdown. His spot on the team was secured.

After the game Howard said simply, "I knew if I got the chance to prove myself, I'd come through."

But neither he nor the Packers could have ever imagined what would transpire during this season.

It really started in the season's third game when Howard returned a punt 65 yards for a touchdown against the San Diego Chargers. Later in the season against the Chicago Bears, he brought a punt back 75 yards for a score, and two weeks later he'd add a 92-yard score against the Lions.

More to the point, he seemed to have returns every week that, if they didn't result in a score, would set up the Packers in great field position and the offense would take it from there.

For the season, Howard returned 58 punts for 875 yards, an NFL record, and he averaged a staggering 15 yards per return. He also averaged another 21 yards per kickoff return.

Offense. Defense. Special teams. Coaching. A fearsome home-field advantage at Lambeau Field. The Packers had everything, and they rolled to a 13–3 record in which the poorest game they played was, you guessed it, in Dallas—a 21–6 setback to the defending Super Bowl champion Cowboys.

But the Packers knew the three games they lost—to Minnesota, Kansas City, and Dallas—were not because they weren't good enough. They had made uncharacteristic mistakes and not executed properly, and the results were predictable.

After that loss to the Cowboys in mid-November, Green Bay went on a tear, winning their last five games and outscoring their opponents 162–45.

The Packers roared into the playoffs as the NFC's top seed, with a first-round playoff bye and as the prohibitive favorite to win the Super Bowl.

Their first playoff opponent would be the ever-dangerous San Francisco 49ers. The Packers had made their definitive coming-of-age statement the year before when they went to 3Com Park and dismantled the then defending league champions. Now it was the 49ers' turn to come to Green Bay and, they hoped, return the favor.

Indeed, the 49ers, with an arrogance and confidence borne of five Super Bowl titles in the previous 15 years, remained unimpressed.

Tight end Brent Jones, who never missed an opportunity to tweak the Packers, told the Green Bay media contingent days before the game, "Everybody's ready to hand the Super Bowl to the Packers. They haven't won anything yet."

And while the Packers had to agree, they also knew that was about to change.

The division playoff dawned with January weather most of the Packers had not seen before. Yes, it was cold and it was nasty. But instead of snow, a cold, relentless rain came down. It began early in the morning and did not subside until late in the day. Sheets of rain made the field a muddy quagmire and a steady wind would play havoc with the passing game, so both teams knew their offenses would be operating at something less than peak efficiency.

The difference was the Packers had Brett Favre, a relentless defense, and Desmond Howard to return kicks. The 49ers were crippled on both sides of the ball, mostly in the form of their dynamic quarterback Steve Young, who had cracked two ribs the week before in a playoff win over the Eagles. Claiming before the game the ribs were just sore and he'd be fine, he was far from it. And after two ineffective, and painful, series, he went to the sidelines in favor of backup Elvis Grbac.

But by then it was already too late because Desmond Howard had, one more time, tilted the field in Green Bay's favor.

After the 49ers' first unproductive drive, Howard fielded a punt at his own 29 and, while it was assumed the miserable field conditions would negate his effectiveness, Howard didn't share that assumption.

"It was a returnable kick," Howard said in the postgame press conference. "I just tried to take it up the middle."

And so he did. As San Francisco tacklers sloshed through the muck trying to take Howard down, he glided through it all as though it was a sunny day on a perfect track, racing 71 yards for the touchdown. It was his fourth return of a kick for a touchdown on the season, and whatever suspense there might have been in the game was quickly diminished.

But for good measure, he sent another charge around Lambeau Field barely five minutes later. Having clearly not learned their lesson from the previous punt, the 49ers again kicked straight to Howard, who returned this kick 46 yards before he was tripped up on a shoestring tackle at the San Francisco 7. Two plays later Favre hit Andre Rison for a touchdown and 14–0 a Packers lead.

The Packers could not have dreamed of a better start.

"Desmond's returns definitely made a difference in the game," Favre said afterward. "It may have made the difference all day."

The Packers continued to dominate, turning a Craig Newsome interception into an Edgar Bennett touchdown run and a 21–0 cushion.

But apparently in an effort to keep fans interested on such a lousy day, Green Bay committed two uncharacteristic special-teams blunders that suddenly turned a potential rout into something far more uncertain than it should have been.

Another 49ers punt late in the second quarter bounced off Packers special-teams star Chris Hayes, who was downfield preparing to block for another Howard return. The free ball was recovered by the 49ers' Curtis Buckley at the Packers 26 and eventually resulted in a Grbac–to–Terry Kirby touchdown pass with just eight seconds left in the half.

It got more interesting as the third quarter began, and again, it was directly attributable to the horrible weather.

At halftime every Packer ditched his muddy, soaked uniform for clean, dry duds for the second half. But Howard was late in changing his uniform, and by the time he was done, the team had already gone back on the field and were ready to take the third-quarter kickoff.

But Howard wasn't there to take his familiar spot alongside Don Beebe. Rison sprinted on the field to take Howard's place, but the

49ers kickoff came up short, squirted between both Rison and Beebe, and since no player had touched the ball, it was again a free ball. San Francisco's Steve Israel fell on the ball at the Packers 4 right about the time Howard emerged from the tunnel to witness what was happening.

He reached the sideline, and the thermonuclear glare from Holmgren was one Howard said he would never forget.

The 49ers took advantage of the gift and scored another touchdown. Now it was a game. Except it really wasn't.

Engineering a 12-play, 72-yard drive that chewed up eight minutes on the clock, Favre threw just two passes and mostly relied on Bennett's running to wear down the 49ers' defense. In the end it resulted in another Packers touchdown and a 28–14 lead. Sanity had been restored.

Despite some uncharacteristic mistakes and the worst weather several players said they had ever played in, Green Bay prevailed, 35–14.

It was another signal that the Packers had not only taken their place among the NFL's best teams, they had taken over the top spot.

"I think we deserve respect now, the respect the 49ers weren't giving us," tight end Mark Chmura said in the book *Titletown Again*. "I think we're a good team and beating the 49ers three times in one year? You tell me. They're a good team and we'll admit they are. But I think we are, too."

Now, for the second straight year, the Packers were back in the NFC championship, but the foe they all wanted to meet wouldn't be joining them.

The Dallas Cowboys, Green Bay's seemingly eternal tormentor, was supposed to dispose of the upstart Carolina Panthers in their divisional playoff, setting up a rematch at Lambeau, where the Packers, and their rabid fans, were convinced retribution would be exacted after too many years of heartache.

In fact, in the waning seconds of Green Bay's dissection of the 49ers, the chant "We want Dallas" coursed through the bowl.

But it didn't quite work out that way. The day after Green Bay's win, the Cowboys traveled to Charlotte, North Carolina, for their expected victory waltz. But the Panthers, with a strong defense and a fairly sizable chip on their shoulders, intercepted Dallas quarterback Troy Aikman three times and went on to a shocking 26–17 win.

"I know Packers fans wanted the Cowboys," Carolina quarterback Kerry Collins said in the press conference days before the conference championship. "I understand that completely because it's become such a great rivalry. But you know what? We beat the Cowboys and we're here."

And the Packers knew they could take no one for granted. After all, the Panthers had done what the Packers were unable to do in their last seven attempts—beat the Cowboys. So that accomplishment alone was more than enough for the Packers to take seriously.

But there was still something inevitable about the result. It would be a game played in perfect Packers weather—three degrees with a windchill of minus-17—on a field resodded and remade after last week's deluge tore it to shreds. These were the circumstances the Packers had wanted and now it was here, laid out before them for the taking.

But the Packers sputtered early. Favre was intercepted by Panthers linebacker Sam Mills, which led to a quick touchdown and a 7–0 Panthers lead.

After that pick, Carolina linebacker Lamar Lathon walked past Favre and taunted him.

"It's gonna be a long day, Brett," he said. "A long day."

After the game Favre smiled at the remark.

"If I kept making throws like that, he was going to be right," he said.

But he didn't keep making throws like that. In fact, he made only one other major error, a second-quarter fumble that led to a Panthers field goal and a 10–7 lead. From then on, the Packers were relentless.

Green Bay followed with another of their time-consuming drives—15 plays, 71 yards—that ended with a touchdown pass to Antonio Freeman. Two plays later cornerback Tyrone Williams intercepted Collins, which led to a Chris Jacke field goal and 17–10 Packers halftime lead.

And while the Panthers gamely hung with the Packers deep into the third quarter, the inevitability of the situation was palpable. The

Packers were simply too strong. They had prepared for this situation for four years, dealing with setbacks and heartbreak and frustration. They weren't about to let it go now.

Another soul-crushing drive—73 yards, 11 plays—started the third quarter and resulted in a Jacke field goal. From there the Packers tightened the vise just a little more.

And when Edgar Bennett sliced into the end zone untouched late in the third to give the Packers a 27–13 advantage, it was all but over.

Green Bay dominated the game on both offense and defense, rolling up 479 total yards to Carolina's 251. Favre completed 19 of 29 passes for 292 yards and two touchdowns, while Bennett ran for 99 yards and a score.

Added to the offensive arsenal was Dorsey Levens, the third-year back who had been plagued by injuries his first two seasons and had yet to unveil the skill the Packers knew he had.

In the most important game in years for the Packers, Levens had the game of his life. He rushed for 88 yards on just 10 carries and caught another five passes for 117 yards and a touchdown.

"I thought I would contribute a little bit, but I never dreamed of having a game like this," Levens said in a packed postgame press conference. "This is definitely a career game for me. I'm in the game plan every week, but usually not this much."

As the game ended and it became clear that, for the first time in 30 years, the Green Bay Packers were headed to the Super Bowl, Lambeau seemed to take on a life of its own. The old stadium, the scene of so much history, was rocking. Players embraced and waded into the crowd to thank the fans who had helped make Lambeau such a home-field citadel.

Team president Bob Harlan, who had gone against conventional wisdom five years earlier and gave complete control of the football operations to one man, wept.

"No way in the world did I expect this," he said in *Titletown Again*. "I was so nervous this week. It's been a very upsetting week and I'm just so delighted now. To reach this game means the world to me."

Then he paused.

"Thank God Ron Wolf and Mike Holmgren came to Green Bay," he said.

But the job was not finished and even amid the celebration, everyone knew it.

"The Super Bowl was our goal and now we're there," Freeman said.

You can look back on the games already mentioned in this chapter and make a strong case of their importance in the history of the franchise. But in the final analysis, it's the Super Bowl that supersedes all, and it is Super Bowl XXXI in New Orleans that will take its rightful place in significance—for obvious reasons.

The last time the Green Bay Packers played in the Super Bowl, humans still had not walked on the moon and going online meant waiting to check out at a grocery store. America was still deeply embroiled in an increasingly unpopular war in Vietnam and Richard Nixon was still trying to get Packers coach Vince Lombardi to run as a vice presidential candidate.

The world had changed so much from 1967 to 1996 to the point where the game itself, still just a novelty when Green Bay battered the Oakland Raiders 33–14 in Miami in the second such contest, had erupted into something resembling a national holiday.

For the Packers of 1967, that second Super Bowl was the end of an era and most of the players knew it. They had given everything two weeks earlier to beat the Dallas Cowboys in the epic Ice Bowl, and somehow they found enough inside to handle a very good Raiders team.

But it had come at a cost, and over the course of the next three or four years, those players began to retire or move on to other teams. And Lombardi, the architect of it all, had resigned as Green Bay's coach after that season, then resigned as the team's general manager the year after that, before moving on for one final season to help resurrect the dormant Washington Redskins.

The Packers of 1996? A very different animal. This was a team at the peak of its skills. A team that, some thought, was ready to take over the title as the next great NFL dynasty. And why not?

Brett Favre was the best player in the game and was just 27 years old. His supporting cast on offense—including running backs

Edgar Bennett and Dorsey Levens; linemen Earl Dotson and Adam Timmerman; tight end Mark Chmura; and wide receivers Antonio Freeman, Robert Brooks, and Derrick Mayes were also in the prime of their careers.

The same was true for a record-setting defense that included nose tackle Gilbert Brown; linebackers Brian Williams and Wayne Simmons; cornerbacks Craig Newsome and Doug Evans; and safety LeRoy Butler, who had also developed into perhaps the top playmaking safety in the league.

But even with all that, the job needed to be completed. And standing in the way were the New England Patriots, coached by the already legendary Bill Parcells.

A defensive genius who had led the New York Giants to two Super Bowl titles in five seasons in the late 1980s, Parcells had taken over the Patriots in 1993 and rejuvenated what had been one of the league's sorriest franchises.

They were 2–14 the year before his arrival and just two seasons later, Parcells had the Patriots in the playoffs. Two years after that, they were in a Super Bowl for the first time in 11 years.

He had been around the block more than a few times with opponents who were viewed as the next big thing, and he had usually found a way to cut them down to size.

And while he voiced his respect and admiration for what his good friend Ron Wolf had accomplished with the Packers, he knew they could be beaten, and what better stage to prove it on than in front of the entire football-watching world in the Super Bowl.

His Patriots reached the AFC title game in a not dissimilar way as the Packers. As the conference's second seed, New England dismissed the Pittsburgh Steelers 28–3 in their divisional playoff and fully expected to meet the top-seeded Denver Broncos for the AFC championship.

But as was the case in the NFC, when the expansion Carolina Panthers, in just their second season of existence, upset the Dallas Cowboys, expansion Jacksonville pulled off its own stunner. The Jaguars, who barely qualified for the playoffs as the sixth seed, shocked the Broncos, 30–27.

Ironically, the Jaguars were led by quarterback Mark Brunell, who had been drafted in 1994 by the Packers but learned quickly that he would get no playing time with Favre already in place and was made available for the expansion draft.

The Patriots then rolled over the Jaguars in the AFC title game, forcing four turnovers and winning 20–6.

It would be a contest in New Orleans between two teams who were new to this stage, but the Packers were installed as a staggering 14-point favorite by the oddsmakers.

And not only was Green Bay the betting favorite, it was also the fan favorite. Packer backers swarmed into New Orleans the week leading up to the game, giddy at the prospect of a Packers return to glory, with the added benefit of escaping snowstorms that battered Wisconsin most of that week.

It was also a study in contrasts between the two teams as they dealt with the media frenzy that has come to define what has come to be known as Super Bowl week.

Bill Parcells, never a media charmer in the best of times, was put on edge early that week thanks to a newspaper report that said this would be his last season with the Patriots due to his deteriorating relationship with team owner Robert Kraft.

He fought and snapped at the press most of the week as he tried to prepare for the task of slowing down the Packers (and it turned out, that Super Bowl was his final game with the Patriots as he resigned to take over the following season as coach of the New York Jets).

Meanwhile, the Packers appeared loose and relaxed, reveling in their newfound fame and notoriety. Reggie White, Brett Favre, and Gilbert Brown were engaging and funny in press sessions.

Defensive coordinator Fritz Shurmur, a veteran of more than 20 NFL seasons, grinned and soaked it all in, even nodding his head when one reporter used a *Star Wars* reference and asked if he was the Obi-Wan Kenobi of the Packers defense.

"Sure," he said. "Who's that?"

Even the usually low-key Holmgren found time to enjoy the festivities, arranging with the New Orleans police to get time to ride his motorcycle around town to relax.

"We're here to get a job done," Holmgren said in the final press conference before the game. "But we wanted to enjoy it, too."

They were indeed enjoying most of what was transpiring in New Orleans (aside from the incessant and inane media questions) because these Packers had a confidence that bordered on cocky. They were so sure they would take care of the Patriots that at times Holmgren had to rein them back in.

For example, in one film session with the defense, the usually taciturn and stone-faced linebacker Wayne Simmons burst out laughing as he watched film of the Patriots offense.

"We're going to kick these guys' asses," Simmons said. "Why can't I say that?"

Holmgren glared at his star linebacker and said, "You know why you can't. Don't give them any advantage."

And in truth, it would take a monumental effort from the AFC champs to compete with the Packers—if the Packers played up to their skill level.

Finally, on game day, Holmgren pulled a motivational trick on his team that he had rarely, if ever, done before. He moved a large table into the middle of the locker room and whatever was on the table had been covered with a cloth.

On cue, he pulled the covering away to show a pile of money that, players assumed, totaled $100,000—the amount of money each player would receive for winning the Super Bowl.

"If you're motivated by money, this is what you're looking at," Holmgren told his team. "But I think you guys are motivated by a lot more than money. You know what this is all about and how important it is. I've shown you how to win this game; now go out there and do it."

It was a game that proved to be everything the Packers had hoped for and, yes, expected.

And it began, to the surprise of no one, with a 32-yard punt return by Desmond Howard to the Packers 45-yard line.

Two plays later Favre changed at the line of scrimmage the play Holmgren had called after he saw a Patriots defensive coverage that made his eyes widen and brought a smile to his face.

Under center, he held up one finger to signal that wide receiver Andre Rison would now be the primary receiver. At the snap, Rison blew past cornerback Otis Smith and gathered in Favre's perfectly thrown ball. It was a 54-yard touchdown and Favre ripped off his helmet, yelling wildly and running toward the Packers sideline, where he jumped in the arms of backup quarterback Doug Pederson.

The Packers could not have scripted a better start, and Favre recalled after the game that, all afternoon while waiting for the game, he had been watching repeats of past Super Bowls on TV and saw the same play called by 49ers quarterback Joe Montana when he connected with Jerry Rice in an earlier Super Bowl.

"Same play," he said. "I was hoping I'd be able to run it."

It was a first half that saw the Patriots grab a 14–10 lead after one quarter before Green Bay, with the help of an 81-yard Favre–to–Antonio Freeman touchdown pass, scored 17 unanswered points in the second quarter for a 27–14 halftime lead.

But New England wouldn't go away quietly. Midway through the third quarter, the Patriots pulled with six points on an 18-yard touchdown run by Curtis Martin.

"We felt good about ourselves at that point," cornerback Willie Clay said later. "We knew we were still in the game."

That's when the Patriots kicked off to the Packers and Desmond Howard, again, responded with one of the most memorable plays in Packers history. Though he had done most of his damage all season as a punt returner, teams forgot he could also be devastating returning kickoffs.

"They can roll the dice and kick it to me if they want," Howard had said earlier in the week.

So they did and Howard made them pay. He took the kickoff at his 1-yard line and came straight up the middle. He broke two tackles, eluded another, and was gone.

"There was only the kicker left and he wasn't going to tackle Desmond in the open field," said his return mate Don Beebe. "I looked up and there he goes."

That return sent a charge through the Superdome and after a successful two-point conversion, the Packers held a 35–21 lead. And while there was still a full quarter and a half to play, the realization seemed to hit everyone that this Super Bowl was history.

The Patriots could generate nothing on offense the rest of the game as the Packers defense, led by the rejuvenated Reggie White, hounded Pats quarterback Drew Bledsoe the rest of the evening. Bledsoe threw two interceptions in the fourth quarter, giving him four for the game, and he was sacked on back-to-back plays by White (giving him three for the game), providing the perfect exclamation point to an incredible season.

The Packers had done it, and for the first time since 1967, Green Bay had a world champion.

It was a classic Packers performance despite a game effort by the Patriots, who did shut down the Green Bay running game and sacked Favre five times.

Still, the Packers quarterback completed 14 of 27 passes for 246 yards and two scores. He also ran for another. But while this was a good performance, the great performance was supplied by Howard, who set three Super Bowl records—longest scoring play (the 99-yard kickoff return), kickoff return average (38.5 yards), and punt return yards (90). He also tied another Super Bowl record with 244 combined return yards. And, of course, his kickoff return for a score changed the course of the game—a fact grimly acknowledged by Parcells.

"We were worried about him but we couldn't cancel the game," Parcells told the media afterward. "He really made the plays. Up until that point, I thought we still had an opportunity."

Perhaps the most enduring image of the Packers' postgame celebration was Reggie White, holding the Vince Lombardi Trophy high in triumph, sprinting the length of the field, trailed by dozens of photographers.

It's hard to imagine this win meaning more than it did to the veteran defensive end. He had risked everything coming to the Packers in free agency. More established and, yes, far more successful franchises had offered White the chance to join in free agency, but he stunned the NFL and reshaped the concept of free agency by signing with the Packers, because he had a feeling there was something special brewing in Green Bay (not to mention it was the largest contract offered to him).

It took four seasons but it had finally come to pass, and now Reggie White was part of a Super Bowl winner.

In a poignant postgame media session, White said, "Now I can sit back with my son for years and watch the highlights of this Super Bowl, and he can see his daddy getting three sacks."

But just seven years later, White died suddenly from cardiac arrhythmia brought on by severe cases of sarcoidosis (an enlargement of the lymph nodes) and sleep apnea. He was only 43 years old.

In the locker room after the win, the normally stoic Holmgren broke down—but only a little.

He told his players how proud he was of them, how hard they had worked, and how well they had played. And he said this: "As much as this trophy means to every other team, it means more to us. It's named after Vince Lombardi and it's back where it belongs."

That this game is among the most important in franchise history is obvious. What should have been another of those games, though, should have followed the next season as the Packers, who many, including Ron Wolf, believed were even stronger than the 1996 version, took the field to defend their title.

Winning a Super Bowl was significant and noteworthy, but winning two in a row? That puts you in rarefied air.

To that point, only five teams had won back-to-back Super Bowls: the Miami Dolphins (1972–1973); the Pittsburgh Steelers twice (1974–1975 and 1978–1979); the San Francisco 49ers (1988–1989), the Dallas Cowboys (1992–1993), and, of course, it all began with the Packers in 1966–1967.

The Packers felt they could join that elite list and put themselves in the same category with those long-ago Packers for whom every player on the roster knew the history.

Sure, there were changes. Desmond Howard, who had been given what amounted to a final chance to make it in the NFL by the Packers and responded with a season for the ages, departed for a massive free-agent deal with the Oakland Raiders. And while he would flash brilliance over the next six seasons with three different teams (including a brief return engagement with the Packers in 1999), he would never again recapture what he had produced in that one season in 1996, where every time he touched the ball, he expected to score.

As well, workhorse halfback Edgar Bennett would miss the entire season after rupturing an Achilles tendon, as would cornerback Craig Newsome, who had been such a game changer in 1996. He suffered a knee injury on the second play of the opening game and was lost for the season.

Also, three established veterans who had meant so much to the championship—left tackle Ken Ruettgers, defensive end Sean Jones, and tight end Keith Jackson—all retired, and the most accurate kicker in team history, Chris Jacke, signed a free-agent deal with the Pittsburgh Steelers.

But with change comes new opportunities, and there was always someone new to step in. And the Packers believed they were younger, stronger, and better than they were the previous season. So did the pundits, who tabbed the Packers as the overwhelming favorites to win a second straight title.

Safety LeRoy Butler was so high on this team that he told the assembled Green Bay media during training camp that he thought this team could go unbeaten. They didn't do that, but they did post a second straight 13–3 record that was tarnished by a one-point loss to the Philadelphia Eagles and a still baffling 41–38 loss in Indianapolis to the then-winless Colts.

But the Packers took care of business that season, eliminating the Tampa Bay Buccaneers in the divisional round of the playoffs and then, one more time, going to San Francisco and knocking off the 49ers, earning a trip to San Diego, California, and Super Bowl XXXII.

And if the Packers had been big favorites against the Patriots the year before, they were also as big a favorite to beat the AFC champion Denver Broncos (they were 10-point underdogs), who were quarterbacked by hard-luck John Elway and who had lost three Super Bowls to the New York Giants, Washington Redskins, and 49ers by an average score of 44–13.

Few figured this would be any different. But it was.

The Packers came in confident, bordering on arrogant, and several players admitted afterward they did not respect the game, the surroundings, or their opponent as much as they should have.

And it cost them. The Broncos did not rely on Elway to beat the Packers. They instead used the running of Terrell Davis, who gained 157 yards on 30 carries and scored three touchdowns despite missing nearly the entire second quarter with a migraine headache.

The Broncos' physical defense also shut down the Packers, holding them to 10 second-half points and forcing three turnovers.

After the game a jubilant Elway held the Lombardi Trophy over his head and his teammates celebrated.

Broncos owner Pat Bowlen told the crowd simply, "This one's for John."

In the Packers locker room, there was bewilderment and despair and realization that a chance for NFL history was over. It was a fact acknowledged by Ron Wolf, who famously told the gathered media afterward, "We're nothing but a fart in the wind."

Even years later that loss remains with Wolf.

"I still can't get over that loss," he said recently. "It's the difference between a very good team and a great team. We could have been a great team."

That game could well be viewed as the high-water mark for the Packers under Wolf and Holmgren. The following season Green Bay began to slip as a new NFC Central power rose—the high-scoring Minnesota Vikings—who beat the Packers twice and posted a 15–1 record to Green Bay's 11–5 mark.

Front-office tension was building as well. Wolf remained the great and powerful Oz and Holmgren, after seven strong seasons, was ready to spread his wings and take on general manager duties, for which he was certain he was now qualified.

Wolf wasn't ready to share power and Holmgren wanted something more. It was a clash of egos, power, and hubris that neither would win.

Just days after the 1998 season ended with a crushing last-second playoff loss to the 49ers, Holmgren announced he was leaving the Packers to take over as head coach and general manager of the Seattle Seahawks.

It was not necessarily unexpected, even though Holmgren's agent, Bob LaMonte, had said only a week earlier that his client was going nowhere. But one more time, a Packers era had ended with a coach deciding to move on.

And while it was certainly not the same as 1968 when a mentally and physically exhausted Vince Lombardi stepped away and his hand-picked successor, Phil Bengtson, took over, Packers fans knew how that worked out and now they braced for what was to come.

Still, Wolf had a track record of making good decisions at the most important times, and when he tabbed Ray Rhodes as Holmgren's successor barely three days later, most were ready to assume he had made the best choice.

"He's the right guy for this time," Wolf said rather cryptically at the January press conference. "He'll provide a little electrical shock for the players."

It was a not-so-thinly veiled reference to the belief that, after seven seasons, players had begun to tune out Holmgren's message. As well, the relationship between Wolf and Holmgren, two driven and successful men with massive egos, had begun to fray. Wolf had the kind of control Holmgren wanted, and Wolf was not inclined to give up the power he had earned.

So when Holmgren signed his stunning eight-year deal with the Seahawks, there were more than a few Packers who didn't shed a tear.

"The Holmgren era is over," veteran safety LeRoy Butler told the *Milwaukee Journal Sentinel.* "[Ray] will be his own man and he'll let everyone else be their own man. It's time for Ray to take over. I think the team will be tougher. I think last year we had a lot of games where we weren't tough and physical enough. I know that's something he will stress and something we need."

But it would prove to be far more complicated than that.

A defensive whiz who had just been fired as head coach of the Philadelphia Eagles, Rhodes was coming to a team where he'd had less than an ideal experience.

Hired as Holmgren's defensive coordinator when Holmgren first came to Green Bay in 1992, Rhodes lasted just two seasons with the Packers. He cited how uncomfortable his family felt in the overwhelmingly white community and returned to the 49ers as defensive coordinator.

In 1995 he took over as the Eagles head coach and after initial success, the positive result faded and he was let go after four seasons.

But Wolf was convinced Rhodes was the right man for a Packers team he believed still had the talent to compete for another Super Bowl. It would be one of the few times Wolf's uncanny ability to spot talent failed him. Rhodes seemed overmatched and uncertain, and the toughness Wolf expected to see was instead replaced by poor execution and inexplicable mistakes.

After a 3–1 start, the Packers went to Denver and were routed by the Broncos. Two weeks later Holmgren brought his new Seahawks team into Lambeau Field and blasted the Packers 27–7. That may well have already signaled the beginning of the end for Rhodes in Green Bay.

As well, Brett Favre, who had such a unique relationship with Holmgren, seemed to regress. He threw for more than 4,000 yards but his completion percentage of 57 percent was his worst as a Packer; his 22 touchdown passes were his lowest since 1993 and his 23 interceptions marked the first time he'd thrown more picks than TDs since 1993.

Yet, amazingly, the Packers still had a shot at the playoffs after beating the Arizona Cardinals in the season finale. But Green Bay's final 8–8 record, its first nonwinning season since 1991, would ultimately not be enough to reach the postseason and, in another stunning move, on the day after the season ended, Wolf fired Rhodes and his entire staff.

Admitting he'd made a mistake and unwilling to compound that mistake by moving forward with a coach he now no longer trusted, Wolf decided to cut the cord.

"Is he a different coach than I thought he was?" Wolf said at the press conference announcing the decision. "Well, yes. What I think we have to have here is a well-disciplined, tough, hard-nosed football team. That's the way you're successful in this business. We have to develop that. We have to get that here. We don't have that here."

For his part, Rhodes was philosophical.

"Things happen for a reason," he said simply.

In a matter of two seasons, the Packers had gone from Super Bowl favorite to a playoff also-ran. They had lost one coach and fired another, and a roster that had been carefully constructed to win and win often was changing rapidly.

"We have a lot of work to do," Wolf said.

And while that was certainly true, it would also become clear with all the changes looming, Ron Wolf would be among them.

Barely two years after Holmgren left in frustration, Wolf announced his retirement as general manager and vice president of the Packers. It was a decision, Wolf said to a packed press conference in February 2001, that he made months earlier and made clear to team president Bob Harlan.

"I was brought here to win," Wolf said at the time. "If it was all about evaluating football talent, I could stay. But now, there's more to it than that. They have to have the best possible people doing for them what needs to be done, when it needs to be done. And I can't give them that anymore. I just hit a wall. It was time."

Now, the two major architects of Green Bay's renaissance were gone—Holmgren to Seattle and Wolf to retirement—and the Packers' future looked as uncertain as it had in many years.

Ray Rhodes had not worked out as Holmgren's replacement as head coach and he had been replaced by Mike Sherman, a onetime tight ends coach for the Packers who had spent the past two seasons with Holmgren in Seattle.

This would be Wolf's last major hiring decision, and the gut feeling he had about Rhodes's hiring also guided him with Sherman.

Packers fans could still be comforted by the thought that with as many changes as there were swirling around them, all would be well as long as Brett Favre remained as quarterback. After all, he would keep the universe in order and provide the stability and quality they had come to expect. Right?

CHAPTER TEN

"THIS IS AARON'S TEAM NOW"

MINNESOTA VIKINGS 38, PACKERS 26

NOVEMBER 1, 2009

Aaron Rodgers and Brett Favre after the Vikings beat the Packers 38–26 on *Monday Night Football.* AP PHOTO/BEN LIEBENBERG

CHAPTER

"THIS IS KARON'S TEAM NOW"

MINNESOTA VIKINGS 30, PACKERS 26

NOVEMBER 1 2020

THIS MAY BE THE GAME THAT MOST PACKERS FANS WILL HAVE THE hardest time including on a list of the most important games in franchise history. But hear me out and please follow along because its importance, I believe, will be made clear in due time.

Yes, concessions will be that this was not a playoff game; it was not a game that changed team history; it was not a game with dramatic historical plays that people have talked about decades later; it was not a game that decided a division championship or a game that any NFL fan even remembers.

It was, quite simply, a regular-season game tucked halfway into an otherwise routine campaign, the result of which would be logged into an otherwise mundane database of endless numbers.

Or was it? Think back and remember that this otherwise forgettable regular-season game at Lambeau Field was anything but and the circumstances, drama, and stunning twists that led to this game were certainly memorable enough.

Let's set the stage, then go back in time before returning once again to this game, and perhaps you'll also come to the conclusion that this game was a lot more important than might have been originally imagined.

It was, in the most basic terms, Brett Favre's return to Lambeau Field—but not as a member of the Green Bay Packers. He had been traded prior to the 2008 season to the New York Jets, where he spent basically one miserable season for a team and a coach he did not really want to play for.

He then retired (more on this to come) again before being lured back by the division rival Minnesota Vikings—a move that enraged Packers fans and delighted their purple-clad neighbors to the north.

Now on this early November night (it was *Monday Night Football*'s highest-rated game, by far, that season), Favre was returning to the place he had spent 16 seasons and became a living legend to Packers fans. And Favre admitted afterward that he had never been more nervous before a game.

That was one side. On the other was Aaron Rodgers, the former first-round draft pick of the Packers who had apprenticed for three seasons under Favre before taking over in 2008 as the starter.

But despite a strong first season as the starter when he threw for more than 4,000 yards and 28 touchdowns, the Packers finished 6–10 and missed the playoffs for the third time in four seasons. There remained, for many Packers fans, a Brett Favre hangover and nothing that Rodgers could do, it seemed, would shake the belief that the only man who belonged under center for the green and gold was Favre.

So, when Favre visited Lambeau Field on this night to take on the man who replaced him, the drama was . . . significant.

And we will come back to this game and the reasons for its overall importance after we go back and examine why this all transpired in the first place.

It can be traced initially to five years earlier when Favre first hinted that he was thinking about retirement. It was nothing serious, mind you, just a thought that it might be time to do something else.

The statement reverberated around the NFL and certainly through Green Bay and Wisconsin and Packers fans across the country. Was he serious? No one really knew, but just the thought of Favre walking away from football and the Packers had sent fans into major panic mode.

But Favre did not follow through with his idle musings, citing the belief that he still had plenty left in his tank and still had plenty to accomplish on the field.

Perhaps coincidentally, however, the Packers organization was also thinking about life after the most prodigious and mercurial quarterback the franchise had ever known. After all, Favre was no kid anymore and he had taken more hits than most quarterbacks. He was still operating at a high level but how long would that continue?

The Packers had brought in a boatload of quarterbacks over the years to back up Favre. But he never left the starting lineup, so these quarterbacks, all seeking an opportunity of their own to play, departed. They included the likes of Ty Detmer, Mark Brunell, Aaron Brooks, and Matt Hasselbeck, who would all go on to start, and play well, for other NFL teams.

But now Favre was 36 years old and the mileage on his body was significant. It was time to draft a quarterback who could take over when Favre finally decided it really was time to step away.

So in the 2005 NFL Draft, in a stroke of kismet that always seems to follow the Packers, a highly touted, record-setting young quarterback from the University of California still had not been selected by the time the Packers chose in the 24th spot of the first round. Aaron Rodgers was supposed to have been one of the first 10 players taken in the draft, but as each name came off the board, Rodgers grew more agitated and resentful.

But when it came to Green Bay's pick, they did not hesitate and selected Rodgers. Here was their future quarterback, though no one in the organization had asked Favre his opinion. That lack of communication would become an issue.

Over the next three seasons, Rodgers would see scant playing time—not unlike the quarterbacks who had preceded him. And Favre, who had often grown close personally with his backups, did not have that same relationship with Rodgers. He was, after all, the first real challenger to Favre's primacy as Green Bay's once and future quarterback.

Then came the bombshell. After several years dropping hints, in March 2008, two months after a devastating NFC Championship Game loss to the New York Giants in which he threw an interception that led to the overtime defeat, Favre held a press conference to announce he was retiring.

It was a tearful, emotional farewell in which Favre thanked everyone who had helped him. But his statement, "I think I can still play but I'm just not sure I want to," left many quizzical and uncertain just how serious he was.

As it turned out, he was not that serious at all.

Only a few weeks later, he began dropping hints that he wanted to return to the Packers to complete some unfinished business. But the Packers had moved on.

That's because, in part, Aaron Rodgers had shown the organization a tantalizing vision of what might be in the season just concluded.

In a road game against the Dallas Cowboys, Favre had been ineffective and then had to leave the game with an injured elbow. Rodgers stepped in and, in his first real competition since being drafted, completed 18 of 26 passes for 201 yards and also rushed for 30 yards. And though his performance came up short in the 37–27 loss, Rodgers had played with confidence and poise, and it was a sign that, just maybe, the Packers had found their heir apparent.

While Favre was back under center the next week, the wheels were turning in the Packers front office about just what the future might hold.

But a wonderful 13–3 season ended with the overtime loss to the Giants, and some in the organization were peeved that Favre did not seem as upset about the defeat as he should have.

Two months later Favre made his announcement. And then the real drama started.

Packers general manager Ted Thompson, who was mentored by Ron Wolf for years, and head coach Mike McCarthy had taken Favre at his word and handed the starting quarterback job to Rodgers. It seemed like a seamless transition. Throughout the spring and into the summer, however, Favre agonized about his future. He already knew he wanted to play again, and if he could, he wanted to return to the Packers.

But Favre said to *Sports Illustrated*'s Peter King at the time that Thompson wasn't likely to explore that possibility.

"Ted told me, 'Aaron's our starter,'" Favre said to King. "I asked if I could compete for the job. He said, 'That is not an option.' He said, 'Coming up there obviously is not good. Things have changed. We've moved on.' He basically said, 'You're not going to play here.'"

But Favre was undaunted. Sensing he still had Packers fans on his side, he wanted to press Thompson to the very limit he could, and on the night before a preseason game, Favre flew back to Green Bay to seek an audience with Thompson and essentially plead for an opportunity to compete for the job he'd held for 16 years.

But Thompson was unmoved. "This is Aaron's team now," he told Favre.

More to the point, Favre was still under contract so he could not seek work with another team as a free agent unless the Packers released him—which they would not do. Instead, on August 7, 2008, Favre was traded to the New York Jets for a conditional draft pick (which ended up being a third-round selection in the 2009 draft).

It was a wonderful, if somewhat unexpected, windfall for the Jets, a team on the verge of being a solid AFC title contender. And even though head coach Eric Mangini was not thrilled with adding a loose cannon like Favre to his roster, he accepted him and hoped for the best.

"I felt like we had a great story to tell," Mike Tannenbaum, the Jets general manager at the time, told ESPN. "Great people in the organization and a good team. I was hoping to get our day in court and let Brett see what we had to offer."

So Favre was officially gone, traded ignominiously to a team he knew nothing about in a conference unfamiliar to him. And the Packers' starting quarterback job—one of the most prestigious and highly scrutinized in sports—belonged to Aaron Rodgers.

As stated, Rodgers had a good first season as the quarterback as he shrugged off the boos from the Lambeau Field faithful and produced some quality performances. But Green Bay managed just a 6–10 record.

It wasn't appreciably better for Favre in New York. He did throw a career-best six touchdown passes in a Week 4 win over the Arizona Cardinals, but for the season, he threw for 3,472 yards with 22 touchdowns and 22 interceptions. The Jets lost four of their final five games, finished 9–7, and missed the playoffs as well. Favre and Mangini never did see eye to eye throughout the season, and Mangini was fired a day after the season ended.

As well, Favre, disheartened and still angry at the Packers, retired again. But this time he was released from the retired-released list by the Jets, making him a free agent and eligible to sign with whichever team he chose.

He was lured out of retirement again, and this time he signed with the Vikings, who had developed into perhaps the Packers' most heated and hated rival. And any goodwill Favre had accumulated from sympathetic fans regarding how he had been treated by Green Bay the previous year quickly evaporated. Packers fans were stunned, hurt, and angry. The only thing that might have infuriated Packers fans more was if he had signed with the Chicago Bears. But the Vikings? That was bad enough.

And while there were a few fans who understood, even sympathized, with Favre's situation and cursed the Packers front office for letting him get away, most fans seethed with rage. Words like "traitor" and "backstabber" were heard everywhere, and the ubiquitous Packers no. 4 jerseys worn seemingly forever by Favre fanatics over the years were burned in disturbing little neighborhood ceremonies around Wisconsin. Was that going a little too far? Of course, but it also showed the level of anger, hurt, and betrayal felt by Packers fans.

Which brings us to this 2009 game at Lambeau Field.

The two teams had already faced off a month earlier at the Metrodome in Minneapolis and Favre played well—completing 24 of 31 passes for 271 yards and three scores—as the Vikings notched a 30–23 win.

Favre had admitted to huge nerves in that game, too, because it was the first time since that nasty divorce two years earlier that he had seen many of the guys on the other sideline with whom he had grown so close.

Vikings fans celebrated and taunted their rivals to the east, and the national football media analyzed and dissected that game in ways most early-season games would never be scrutinized. Yes, Favre had played steady, controlled football and kept his emotions in check to deliver a solid performance that would clearly make the Vikings an NFC title contender.

But lost in that game was the fact that, in terms of sheer numbers, Rodgers had outplayed his mentor. Dealing with emotions of his own and still looking for acceptance by fans and teammates alike, Rodgers completed 26 of 37 passes for 384 yards and two touchdowns. He had been harassed and pounded the entire game by a vicious Vikings pass rush that had sacked him eight times, forcing one fumble that led to one touchdown and intercepting him another time that led to another TD.

But Rodgers had hung in, absorbed the punishment and mistakes, and brought the Packers back late to the point where they were within one score of winning before time ran out.

That was just the opening act, and most football fans were waiting for the rematch at the storied NFL venue where Favre had created so much magic and so many memories.

Indeed, the history was long. The hurt was deep. And for the first time, Favre wasn't sure what to expect from Packers fans as he ran onto the field wearing purple.

He found out soon enough. The boos cascaded down from the highest reaches of the stadium.

Signs were everywhere proclaiming Favre, again, as a "traitor," "Judas," and "Drama Queen." One sign derisively welcomed Favre back as "Brent." Earlier a plane flew over Lambeau Field with a sign trailing it saying "Retire No. 4 Forever." So, yeah, there were some hard feelings and even a veteran of nearly 20 NFL seasons like Favre was not immune.

"Yeah, I was nervous," Favre admitted afterward.

But his head coach, Brad Childress, downplayed all the drama in the postgame press conference.

"Yes, he was nervous but it wasn't like he was curled up in the fetal position in the locker room or anything," Childress said.

Again, Favre kept his emotions in check and delivered a solid performance, leading the Vikings to a 24–3 lead midway through the third quarter that silenced the hostile crowd and made more than a few wonder what the Packers might have been like if he were still under center.

But what may have gone unnoticed at the time was that Rodgers, again, outplayed Favre—at least statistically. Undaunted by the Vikings performance, Rodgers led the Packers back with 17 straight points, closing the deficit to 24–20 by the end of the quarter.

Favre responded with two more touchdown passes in the fourth quarter and Minnesota prevailed, 38–26. And when it was over, Favre left the field, his hand raised in triumph and perhaps a little defiance as well. He had come into the proverbial lion's den and left not only unscathed but victorious. He completed 17 of 28 passes for 244 yards and four touchdowns. He did not throw an interception in either meeting against his former team.

Once again, Rodgers was battered by the Vikings' relentless defense, chased all evening and sacked five times. But again, he withstood the pressure, completing 26 of 41 passes for 287 yards and three touchdowns. He also rushed for 51 yards.

The postgame attention was mostly focused on Favre, who relished what he had accomplished.

"I had mixed emotions coming in, because I know how special these fans are," Favre said afterward. "I want to lead this Vikings team to a Super Bowl, believe me, I do. And I will do everything in my power. But I also know the Packer fans are what make this organization so special, unique, and that will never change. How could you not miss that?"

Asked where this game ranked among his many victories, Favre smiled and said, "This is right up there."

For Rodgers, it was a learning experience as well as an opportunity to prove, under remarkably difficult circumstances, that he most certainly belonged as the Packers quarterback. In both meetings against the Vikings, he had been pounded almost without pause and yet he posted big numbers and nearly pulled off wins in both games. Indeed, he left the game in Lambeau limping and battered in just about every way imaginable.

"I'll be OK in a couple of days," Rodgers said in the press conference afterward. "This one will hurt for a couple of days, though, physically and mentally."

But he showed the maturity and calm that would serve him well in the years to come when he was asked about the duel with Favre.

"I hate losing to whoever's at quarterback for them," he said. "I hate losing to the Vikings. We had our chances but in the end it just wasn't enough."

So that was that. The Packers-Favre drama had ended with Favre and the Vikings winning both rounds. And both sides had moved on— or at least made the attempt.

"Hopefully we'll get another crack at these guys down the road," Packers' coach Mike McCarthy said.

But they wouldn't.

Favre would go on to post perhaps the best season of his long and distinguished career. Everything fell together that season for the Vikings and for their leader. Favre would lead last-minute comebacks and throw incredible passes and bond with his new teammates and Vikings fans, who reveled in his heroics while knowing full well Packers fans were watching green with envy and red with fury.

Favre completed a career-best 68 percent of his passes while throwing for 4,202 yards, which was topped only by his 1995 and 1998 seasons in Green Bay. He also threw just seven interceptions, and his interception percentage that season was by far the best of his career.

And the Vikings flourished, posting a 12–4 record and earning the no. 2 seed in the NFC playoffs. The Vikings advanced in the playoffs when Favre threw four touchdown passes in a 34–3 rout of the Dallas Cowboys.

But eventually, as Packers fans have known forever, there would come a time sooner or later when Brett Favre would revert to Brett Favre. And this time it came at the absolute worst time.

Beaten and harassed all game by the New Orleans Saints in the NFC Championship Game, Favre nonetheless persevered. Now, with the game tied 28–28, Favre was driving the Vikings into Saints' territory in the final minute for what figured to be the game-winning field goal and a trip to the Super Bowl.

But with just 19 seconds remaining and facing third down and 15 yards to go on the Saints' 38-yard line, Favre rolled right and, despite an open field where he could have run to gain at least 10 yards if not the first down, he threw back across the field and his pass was intercepted by Saints cornerback Tracy Porter. It was, unfortunately for the Vikings, vintage Favre—a poor decision at the worst time in an effort to make a big play.

Vikings fans were horrified and furious. Packers fans? They looked on, smiled, and said, "Tell us something we don't know." It was what you accepted with the force of nature that was Brett Favre.

The game went into overtime and the Saints won it with a field goal and went on to win the Super Bowl. Favre returned to the Vikings the following season but wasn't the same. He struggled on the field, injuries began to pile up, and by the end of the season, Favre's record-breaking games-started streak would end due to an assortment of injuries. After that season he retired again—this time for good.

Meanwhile, Aaron Rodgers had moved to consolidate his hold on the Packers. For a season and a half, Packers fans had waited, perhaps irrationally, for the front office to come to its senses and somehow bring their hero back to Green Bay.

But they knew what they had in Rodgers and they knew that, given time, he would be every bit the quarterback Favre had been—and perhaps more.

And while Favre was leading the Vikings to the playoffs in 2009, Rodgers was doing the same thing in Green Bay.

After the loss to Minnesota at Lambeau, the Packers won seven of their final nine games, finished 11–5, and earned the fifth seed in the NFC playoffs. And in truth, Rodgers's statistics were almost identical to Favre's—he completed 65 percent of his passes for 4,434 yards, 33 touchdown passes, and seven interceptions.

The Packers lost a wild playoff game—51–45 in overtime to the Arizona Cardinals—in which Rodgers threw for 423 yards and four touchdowns. The torch had been passed and, finally, everyone knew it.

Why was the second loss to the Vikings one of the most important games in team history? It was one of the last, and best, opportunities for Packers fans to measure the past with the future, and while Favre's Vikings had won both meetings, they saw in Rodgers the true heir apparent under center.

Rodgers had absorbed it all—the media glare, the comparisons, the questions, the criticism—and had played Favre to a virtual standstill. The future had arrived in Green Bay and it wasn't the dark, uncertain disaster many people had expected.

And in the 2010 season, an even more confident Rodgers evolved into an even better role model, leader, and quarterback. His Packers beat Favre's Vikings twice and, despite a season rife with injuries to key players, Rodgers led Green Bay to two key end-of-the-season wins, a spot in the playoffs, and eventually the Super Bowl.

As Packers general manager Ted Thompson had said two years earlier, this was now Aaron Rodgers's team. Where it would go from there was anyone's guess.

CHAPTER ELEVEN

"THIS IS OUR TIME"

PACKERS 31, PITTSBURGH STEELERS 25

FEBRUARY 6, 2011

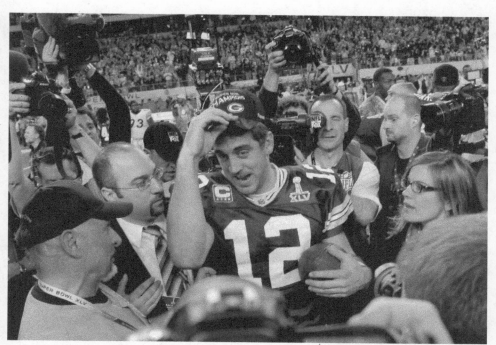

Super Bowl XLV MVP Aaron Rodgers lets it sink in after the Packers beat the Steelers, 31–25.
AP PHOTO/MATT SLOCUM

IT CAME FROM NOWHERE, REALLY. UNLIKE PREVIOUS PACKERS TRIPS to the Super Bowl, all of which seemed to have the air of inevitability, the 2010 Packers seemed to be a crew searching for itself the entire season until the proverbial light switched on at the perfect time and then everything made sense.

On the list of most important wins in franchise history, the case could be made that this one may have been the most important because, for starters, it validated nearly everything the Packers had endured over the previous three years with the Brett Favre drama. It had been a painful, nasty, and, many thought, an unnecessary divorce that had forced the franchise into a decision it didn't have to make.

But that all seemed like ancient history now—and in NFL time it probably was. It was 2010 and Favre had retired yet again, even though the Vikings again made an overture to bring him back.

And in Green Bay, which had struggled with Favre's departure and dreaded what the future might hold without him, Aaron Rodgers was firmly, totally, and completely in command.

There are other reasons why this Super Bowl XLV victory in icy Dallas, Texas, was so vital in the long history of the franchise.

It was a return to the NFL pinnacle that many Packers fans, as well as many longtime NFL observers, had thought was too far in the past. Yes, free agency and revenue sharing had kept the Packers solvent and competitive, but there was a belief that the best of the Packers, days were behind them. After all, if Green Bay could only win one Super Bowl with a generational talent like Brett Favre, there had to be some foundational issues.

As well, the verdict remained in doubt about the game-management skills of head coach Mike McCarthy; the front-office acumen of Ted Thompson, who had learned the game at the right hand of Ron Wolf but had a puzzling disinterest in pursuing free agents; a defense that collapsed at the worst time; and about whether Aaron Rodgers could get over the hump of being a good quarterback who wasn't quite good enough.

Indeed, there was still the vivid memory of the 2009 playoff loss to the Arizona Cardinals, where Rodgers had lit up the desert for 423 passing yards and four touchdowns. But he'd thrown a costly interception, had been sacked five times, and lost a fumble in overtime that ultimately sealed the 51–45 overtime loss.

Rodgers had all the skills needed to lead the Packers to another title, but something was missing and no one really knew if that ingredient could ever be found. And as the 2010 season progressed, those questions remained.

Nonetheless, it would be one of those seasons in Packers annals that would not soon be forgotten, because it would evolve into a season where nothing came easily. And that's the main reason this is such an important game in the team's history.

It's easy to look back now and say that inevitability pulled up a chair and made itself at home with the Packers on their way to a tight, thrilling Super Bowl win over the Pittsburgh Steelers. But it was anything but that.

Injuries, inconsistency, and uncertainty dogged these Packers for four months. With everything from committing 18 penalties (still a team record through the 2021 season) in an early-season loss to the Chicago Bears to overcoming season-long injury woes that followed them into the Super Bowl, this was a battle from start to finish.

"We have high-character guys on this team," linebacker A. J. Hawk said in the *Milwaukee Journal Sentinel* after beating the Steelers. "It sounds like a cliché but that's the way it was. We just stayed the course."

They stayed that course even after placing 15 players (a league high that season) on season-ending injury reserve. They did it after overcoming disastrous losses to the Miami Dolphins, Washington Redskins, and Detroit Lions. And they did it after losing Rodgers for a game and a half late in the season.

The key came in the final two weeks of the regular season when, quite simply, the Packers had to win those final two games to just qualify for the postseason. That had become necessary the previous two weeks when Rodgers suffered a concussion just before halftime against the Lions. Backup Matt Flynn was unable to generate anything as he took over in the second half and the Packers suffered a shattering 7–3 loss to the moribund Lions.

The next week, facing the always-tough New England Patriots on the road and without the still-concussed Rodgers, Green Bay played well but still fell 31–27.

That left the Packers with an 8–6 record and with the mathematical reality that a loss in either of their final two games would mean playoff elimination.

But in what would mark the final turning point in a season of stark detours, Green Bay routed the New York Giants, who faced the same postseason circumstances as the Packers.

Rodgers returned to a raucous Lambeau Field, threw for 404 yards and four touchdowns, and the Packers rolled 45–17.

They had survived their first test and now came the final challenge, beating their old pals the Chicago Bears, who had already clinched the NFC North title.

Again, the math was simple. Beat the Bears and the Packers would clinch the sixth, and final, playoff spot. Lose and they'd need the Giants to lose their finale to the Redskins (which, as it turned out, they would not).

It was desperate, ugly football for the Packers, who had so much to gain, and for the Bears, who played all their starters even though they were already assured of a first-round playoff bye. It was, after all, an opportunity to deliver a shattering loss to the franchise that had tormented them for so long.

In the end the Packers generated just enough offense while the defense was superb. It allowed Chicago's offense just 227 yards and harassed quarterback Jay Cutler all day, sacking him five times and forcing him to throw two interceptions, including one in the final minute as they were driving for a tying touchdown.

Green Bay had accomplished what they needed to do with the 10–3 win, and now they had reached the playoffs where the ubiquitous cliché is that anything could happen. But could it really?

In this case it could, as the Packers, led by Rodgers and a reborn defense, strung together perhaps the most impressive four-game stretch at the most crucial time in the franchise's history.

The Packers had knocked down the NFL's back door and stormed their way into the postseason, but the fact was they were still the sixth, and last, seed. That meant if they were going to reach the Super Bowl, they would have to go on the road and win in three of the unfriendliest venues in the league.

It began in Philadelphia, where the Packers would face the NFC East Division champion Eagles. Featuring a fast, aggressive defense and the offensive playmaking skills of quarterback Michael Vick, the Eagles were looking to avenge a season-opening 27–20 loss to the Packers at Lincoln Financial Field, a normally difficult place for opponents but also where the Eagles lost four times that season.

This would be no different and would send the Packers off on a remarkable road that would be headlined by Rodgers.

In this first-round game, the Packers would run for 138 yards, spearheaded by James Starks's 123 yards on 23 carries. Rogers threw for 180 yards and three touchdowns, and a final Philadelphia drive was thwarted in the closing minutes by a Tramon Williams interception in the end zone. Green Bay prevailed 21–16 and provided Rodgers with his first playoff win as the Packers' starting quarterback.

When asked about that statistical fact after the game, Rodgers was typically low-key.

"I never felt I had a monkey on my back," he said. "It was just good to win."

That victory propelled the Packers to another road engagement, this time at the Georgia Dome in Atlanta against the Falcons, who had secured the NFC's top seed with a 13–3 record. They were rested and ready and confident, and the Packers' improbable jaunt through the playoffs seemed ready to end. After all, the Falcons owned a 7–1 home record and had already knocked off the Packers earlier in the season— winning 20–17 despite a 344-yard passing effort from Rodgers.

But this was the postseason and the Packers had an advantage that the Falcons did not: they had been in a playoff mode for the past month and were playing with a sense of urgency that Atlanta did not understand or expect.

And in a performance Aaron Rodgers called one of the best of his career, Green Bay rolled over the Falcons, 48–21, thanks to a 28-point second-quarter eruption that featured two Rodgers touchdown passes and a 70-yard interception return for another score by Williams.

In all, the Packers hung 35 unanswered points on the bewildered Falcons and a raucous, deafening Georgia Dome crowd was reduced to stunned silence. Rodgers was superb, completing 31 of 36 passes for 366 yards and three touchdowns, calling this "perhaps my best performance. The stage we were on and the importance of the game. It was a good night. I felt like I was in a zone."

So were the Packers, who had hit the road for two tough playoff games and had come out winners each time. Suddenly—in the minds of Packers fans, NFL observers, and the Packers themselves—this was beginning to look like a team of destiny.

And for a team of destiny, perhaps there was no better matchup than to face their ancient rivals—the Chicago Bears—with the winner headed to the Super Bowl.

To many, this was the inevitable and perhaps final step for the Packers to complete their improbable postseason journey.

The two teams, after all, had battled each other since the days of leather helmets. They had played in epic, memorable games over the decades, but due to the vagaries of the schedule, the fact that they had been in the same division seemingly forever, and the relative fortunes of each team over the years, an interesting statistic had developed.

The two teams had never faced each other in an NFL championship game. They had faced each other for a divisional title back in 1941, but with the league or conference championship on the line, this meeting would be a first.

They were evenly matched, too. The Bears were coached by Lovie Smith, who took over in Chicago in 2004 and made it one of his first goals to reverse the horrifying trend in the recent Bears-Packers rivalry. Indeed, since 1992 the Bears had lost 20 of the 24 meetings between the two teams and, quite frankly, many of those losses weren't even close.

But Smith, who had made a name for himself as one of the NFL's top defensive assistant coaches, vowed to end that disastrous stretch with a combination of great defense, superb special teams, and a capable, if often unspectacular, offense.

And it worked. In his seven seasons guiding the Bears, Smith had chalked up three division titles and a trip to the Super Bowl. More importantly, his Bears were 8–6 in regular-season meetings with the hated Packers.

This season they had split their games—the Bears winning at home thanks to a Green Bay team-record 18 penalties and the Packers grinding out a 10–3 win at Lambeau Field in the season finale that secured Green Bay's postseason spot.

The Bears came into the title game confident and loose with a 12–5 record that had included an impressive 35–24 divisional playoff win over the talented Seattle Seahawks the week before, a game in which they had built a 28–3 lead by the third quarter.

On a cold, sunny day at Soldier Field, though, the Packers dominated early, building a 14–0 halftime lead on touchdown runs by Rodgers and James Starks. But had it not been for Packers mistakes—including a Rodgers interception and three dropped passes—it could have been far worse for the home team.

But the Bears were hanging on coming out of the locker room, and the hope was that their talented, if mercurial, quarterback, Jay Cutler, would finally flash the form he had shown much of the season when he threw for more than 3,200 yards and 23 touchdowns.

Unfortunately for Chicago, Cutler had been harassed and hounded much of the first half and it took its toll when, after a second-quarter sack, Cutler apparently injured his knee and did not reveal it to his coaches or teammates.

Determined to gut it out in the third quarter, Cutler simply could not, and after one series, he had to give way to backup Todd Collins. It did not go well.

Collins was simply awful. In two series, one of which was a gift-wrapped opportunity after a Rodgers goal-line interception by linebacker Brian Urlacher was brought back to midfield, Collins looked jittery and unprepared. He threw four straight incompletions, and Lovie Smith had seen enough.

As a last gasp, Smith called on no. 3 quarterback Caleb Hanie, a second-year player who had thrown all of 14 passes in four games as a pro. But as is often the case in pro sports, when something unexpected occurs, something amazing often happens.

Playing with the calm resolve of a veteran, Hanie lit up the Packers defense, directing a 67-yard, eight-play drive that resulted in a Chester Taylor run and cut the Packers' lead in half.

But in this remarkable postseason for Green Bay came one of the most improbable plays in the team's playoff history. On third down and five from his own 15, Hanie tried to hit running back Matt Forte, but Packers' 318-pound nose tackle B. J. Raji had stepped back into pass coverage and intercepted the pass, rumbling 18 yards for the touchdown with just six minutes to play. Chicago again closed to within a touchdown on a Hanie touchdown pass, but a final drive was ended with an interception by cornerback Sam Shields.

"I'm numb," Packers coach Mike McCarthy said in the postgame press conference "Now, we have the opportunity to achieve greatness. This was the path that was chosen for us."

"I'm at a loss for words," Rodgers told the *Milwaukee Journal Sentinel*, which was an achievement in itself.

But as McCarthy said, it was indeed the path that two months earlier had seemed unattainable. But now the Packers were headed to their fifth Super Bowl, this one in Dallas and their first in 13 seasons, and with an opportunity to do something no team had done before. After all, no sixth-seeded playoff team had ever won a Super Bowl. But in this season of improbable occurrences, the Packers knew everything was falling their way.

And that meant a meeting with the AFC champion Pittsburgh Steelers, who had posted a 12–4 regular-season record and earned the AFC's no. 2 seed.

The Steelers, five-time Super Bowl champions and looking to make their third Super Bowl appearance in six seasons, knocked off the Baltimore Ravens, 31–24, in their divisional-round game and then faced the rejuvenated New York Jets, who, like the Packers, were a no. 6 seed making a lot of noise. They had upset both the Indianapolis Colts and New England Patriots in their playoff run before falling behind the Steelers 24–0 at halftime in the title game. But a second-half rally made the game interesting as the Jets outscored the Steelers 19–0 before Pittsburgh held on for the win.

The Steelers counted on the steady play of sixth-year quarterback Ben Roethlisberger, who had thrown for 3,200 yards and 17 touchdowns in 12 games; running back Rashard Mendenhall, who had rushed for 1,273 yards and 13 touchdowns; and perhaps the NFL's best overall defense.

For the Packers, this was just another challenge to overcome, including the kind of weather normally reserved for Wisconsin in February.

The Dallas/Fort Worth area was hammered by ice, snow, and low temperatures that hadn't been in the area in more than 15 years. The awful weather paralyzed the region and forced the cancellation of several Super Bowl–related activities. More than a few Packers watched and smiled as the metroplex slipped and slid and cursed the elements.

"Packers weather," they said simply.

It would prove to be more than that in a game that proved to be a microcosm of a season never to be forgotten. The Packers used their opportunistic defense and another great performance from Aaron Rodgers to overcome more crippling injuries and a last-minute rescue to prevail.

"This is what you work for," said head coach Mike McCarthy, who had absorbed his share of criticism over the years for his sometimes peculiar play calling and conservative approach. "I can't give the players enough credit. We had our bumps in the road but we kept fighting. It was a great team victory."

The Packers jumped out to a 21–3 lead midway through the second quarter when Rodgers threw touchdown passes to Jordy Nelson and Greg Jennings and safety Nick Collins intercepted Roethlisberger and returned the pick for a score.

But the Steelers began their rally and it was aided by the Packers' perpetual foe that season—injuries. On a 37-yard completion to

Antwaan Randle El, cornerback Sam Shields, who had played brilliantly in the postseason, suffered a shoulder injury that sent him to the locker room. He did not return.

Then, on the next play, veteran cornerback Charles Woodson, who had been such a vital and steadying force all season, dove for a pass intended for wide receiver Mike Wallace. It was incomplete and both players landed awkwardly. Wallace got up immediately but Woodson did not.

"I knew the second I landed what had happened," Woodson said afterward. "I heard the crack. I've broken a few things over the years and I knew it was broken."

Indeed, Woodson had suffered a broken left collarbone and was out for the rest of the game. Those two injuries, plus the loss of veteran wide receiver Donald Driver to an ankle injury, left the Packers depleted on both sides of the ball.

At halftime, with Green Bay clinging to a 21–10 lead, Woodson delivered a tear-filled speech to his teammates, talking about how much they'd overcome and that after 13 seasons in the league, this may be his last chance to be a part of something special.

"He tried to give a pep talk and he broke down in tears," Packers' defensive line coach Mike Trgovac told *USA Today*. "He got so emotional it was unreal. It was from the heart."

"I haven't cried that hard since I was kid," Woodson recalled later.

The second half would be a struggle. A Roethlisberger-to-Wallace touchdown pass and the ensuing two-point conversion with seven minutes to play brought Pittsburgh to within 28–25, and the momentum appeared to have shifted.

But in another one of those remarkable plays at the most important of junctures, the Packers came through. Facing third down from their own 25 and the tide clearly turning, Rodgers threw a perfect pass down the middle to a heavily covered Greg Jennings. Despite playing with a dislocated finger, Jennings made the crucial grab for a 31-yard gain.

The Packers held on to the ball until nearly the two-minute mark of the game when Mason Crosby kicked a 23-yard field goal that provided a badly needed cushion.

The Steelers could do nothing on their final possession, and the Packers could celebrate the 31–25 victory.

Of the Packers' four Super Bowl victories, perhaps none meant as much as this one, given everything they had overcome.

"We have a lot of high-character guys on this team," Rodgers said in the postgame press conference.

For McCarthy, it was the perfect conclusion to a challenging season.

"No disrespect to the Steelers [but] we fully expected to win this game," McCarthy said in the postgame press conference. "This was our time. That was the last thing I told them when we broke the team meeting: 'This is our time. It's time to bring the Lombardi Trophy back to Green Bay.'"

"It was a special night," said Rodgers, who completed 24 of 39 passes for 304 yards and was named the game's most valuable player. "We've been through a lot this year. To be able to finish it like this was really something special."

It was indeed special and, at least for the next 10 years, it was a feeling that would not be repeated for the Packers.

Despite having one of the game's premier quarterbacks and the resources to build perhaps another NFL dynasty, Green Bay has not returned to the Super Bowl despite having several tantalizing opportunities to do so.

Much has transpired in the time since that triumphant night in Arlington, Texas, and it has tested the faith and resilience of even the most ardent fan.

But there is a history in Green Bay and plenty of scar tissue built up over decades of victory and defeat, of close calls, soaring optimism and debilitating loss. And it is all part of the narrative of the Green Bay Packers, a franchise that lived on a knife's edge for years before evolving into one of the iconic sports franchises in the American sports landscape.

It has never been easy but, as Vince Lombardi would probably say, nothing worthwhile ever is. So the Packers will move forward, continue to defy the odds, play the kinds of games that will be remembered down through the ages, and continue to show generations of fans that through good times and bad, the Packers endure.

And that's always a story worth telling.

EPILOGUE

THESE GAMES WERE PRETTY SIGNIFICANT, TOO

I'VE CHOSEN THE GAMES THAT I BELIEVE BEST DESCRIBE THE ARC OF Green Bay Packers history over more than a century. It wasn't easy, and I had to leave many significant games off the list.

That's what this section will examine—or at least attempt to examine. The following games may not have changed the course of the Packers as a franchise, but they were awfully close or, in a couple of cases, they were just flat-out memorable games that Packers fans still talk about today. These are in no particular order and are certainly open for debate.

Enjoy.

IN THE BEGINNING
Packers 7, Minneapolis Marines 6
October 23, 1921

This is where it all started. What would be would be. The future stars, the great games, the championships, and the heartbreaks and triumphs, they were all to follow.

The formation of the Green Bay Football Team came in 1919, and by 1921 it had already established itself as a regional force. As well, the game itself had found a level of interest that led to the formation of the American Professional Football Association, which would be renamed a year later as the National Football League.

But that was for another day and another time. In 1921 the Packers were still looking to prove themselves as a team to be taken seriously in a new league. So when they opened their first APFA season, Curly Lambeau already knew the significance. For two years his team had beaten up on what amounted to a collection of former high school and college players who gathered for the fun of continuing to play football.

Lambeau had bigger goals in mind for his team. So this first season of "professional" football would be vital, and the first game, to be played at Hagemeister Park in Green Bay, would set the tone.

Indeed, in a publication known as the *Dope Sheet*, the "official" publication of those early Packers, the game against Minneapolis was touted as a battle between league powerhouses—even if such a designation was still to be established.

Said the *Dope Sheet* in anticipation of the league's first game: "The Marines have conceded that they expect to face as dangerous an opponent as they have met so far and also realize that theirs and the Packers claim to a crack at the championship teams depends very largely upon results next Sunday."

According to observers, a crowd of 6,000 squeezed into Hagemeister to watch the two teams collide, and it would be a typical, physical, low-scoring affair.

Ben Dvorak would score a touchdown to give the Marines a 6–0 lead and they held that advantage until the fourth quarter when Green Bay's Dave Hayes recovered a fumble in Marines territory. Eventually, Art Schmaehl would score the first touchdown in Packers professional history, a four-yard rumble through the middle of the Marines defense. Curly Lambeau would add the pivotal extra point and the Packers escaped with a 7–6 victory.

The hyperbole afterward was typical of the time as George Calhoun, the sports editor of the *Green Bay Press-Gazette* who three years earlier had teamed with Lambeau to create the new team, wrote:

"In the greatest game of football ever seen on a Green Bay gridiron, the Packers celebrated their entrance into the Professional Football league by taking the far-famed Minneapolis Marines into camp to the tune of 7–6 before a crowd that jammed every corner of the field at Hagemeister Park."

The journey had begun for a franchise in which no one could predict what would ensue. But it was a great start.

As for this being a championship preview, it wasn't even close. The APFA would feature 21 teams that season, including such anachronisms as the Washington Senators, Detroit Tigers, Cincinnati Celts, and Canton Bulldogs. There were also teams from Evansville, Indiana; Rock Island, Illinois; Dayton, Ohio; and Tonawanda, New York.

The Packers would finish seventh that season with a 3–2–1 record. The Marines finished just 1–3–1 as Chicago, with a 9–1–1 mark, "won" the league title, a half-game ahead of Buffalo.

In June 1922 the AFPA was renamed the National Football League and featured 18 teams, including a team registered as the "Green Bay Blues." Lambeau, who had always hated the name Packers, wanted a change, but when every other team in the new NFL continued to refer to them as the Packers, Lambeau relented a year later and returned to the name that would become one of the most identifiable in American sports.

END OF AN ERA, PART III
San Francisco 49ers 30, Packers 27
January 3, 1999

Sports dynasties sometimes die quietly and without complaint. There is a realization that time and age and injury and bad decisions have exacted their cost, and it was time to face the fact that years of domination and excellence would have to end.

Sure, some ended dramatically and quickly, but others have simply worn down like an old furnace that simply couldn't provide the needed warmth any longer.

This was the case for the Packers' first dynasty. In a remarkable period from 1936 to 1944, the Packers won three NFL championships, lost a fourth, and won five division titles (and never finished worse than second).

Under the charismatic and demanding leadership of Curly Lambeau, the Packers were the team to beat year after year, and it was a reputation the organization, and the fans, guarded jealously.

But after outlasting the New York Giants 14–7 to win the 1944 title, the dominance of the Green Bay Packers was about to end, though in truth, no one really knew it at the time.

The realization would hit slowly and methodically, and events both on the field and off would destroy the foundation and lead to years of decline.

The end of that reign, technically, came in 1945 when Green Bay would post a 6–4 record and third place in the Western Division, its worst showing since 1934. The next two seasons would be no better, with 6–5 and 6–5–1 records.

Then the bottom fell out in 1948, and if there was any doubt that the halcyon days of the Packers had ended, this season put that to rest. Green Bay went just 3–9, and a year later Lambeau would depart in a hail of recrimination and bad blood and anger. The Packers would not enjoy another winning season until 1959.

Which brings us to dynasty no. 2 under Vince Lombardi. His accomplishments are well chronicled and celebrated as he built the Packers into the team of the 1960s, which included five championships in his nine seasons as head coach.

But unlike the Lambeau years where the Packers lost air like an old birthday balloon, these Packers knew the end had come.

Indeed, after winning the second Super Bowl, these battered and aging Packers acknowledged that the best of their days were over, leading the players at halftime of Super Bowl II to give everything they had left for "the old man."

Lombardi would resign as head coach weeks later, and the Packers in 1968 suffered their first losing season since 1958. Two years later Lombardi was dead and the Packers would wander in the NFL wilderness for the better part of the next two decades.

Then came the hope of a third dynasty that, in the final analysis, probably ended before it should have. This, of course, was the partnership of Ron Wolf, Mike Holmgren, and Brett Favre, a triumvirate that would make the Packers, again, the team to beat.

Wolf supplied the players, Holmgren coached them up, and Favre was ringleader for one the NFL's most entertaining and explosive offenses. And from 1993 to 1998, the Packers won one Super Bowl, lost a second, claimed three division titles, and established a standard of excellence that the rest of the NFL looked to copy.

But on a chilly afternoon next to the San Francisco Bay, any thoughts of a Packers regime came crashing down in a controversial and painful loss to the San Francisco 49ers. And not unlike in the Lambeau years when massive egos and demands for more power ended one dynasty, this one ended in a similar fashion and left many Packers fans, and players, to wonder what might have been.

In truth, cracks in the foundation could be seen the year before when Holmgren began to ruminate about what it might be like to not only be head coach but general manager as well. It was not an unreasonable question.

Holmgren had shown his ability as a great coach who could bring the best out of many of his players. He had been around the game a long time and worked closely with Wolf in the drafting of players, and he believed he had reached a point where he could do the backbreaking jobs of both coach and general manager.

Unfortunately for Holmgren, the current general manager was not inclined to abdicate that responsibility. By the time Super Bowl XXXII rolled around and the Packers prepared to face the underdog Denver Broncos, some in the media began to craft a rift between the power-hungry head coach and the intransigent general manager. Both men vigorously denied there were any issues between them, but in the media frenzy that is Super Bowl week, it began to take root.

Did it impact Green Bay's performance in the Super Bowl, where the Packers were expected to roll over the Broncos on the way to their second straight title? Perhaps. But this much is certain—the Packers' 1998 season was more than a little defined by the power struggle that, frankly, did not exist.

The Packers remained a formidable power on the field, led by Favre, who was at the peak of his skills. But as is often the case, when a king rules for too long, there are always challengers ready to take the crown, and by this stage the division rival Minnesota Vikings had grown powerful in their own right.

The Vikings, who had always given the Packers trouble over the years, especially with their rugged defense, had now put together a fearsome offense that included versatile quarterback Randall Cunningham, veteran running back Robert Smith, and explosive wide receiver Cris Carter. But the new X factor was a tall, lanky, athletic, troubled wide receiver named Randy Moss, who many teams would not consider drafting that spring due to his well-documented legal run-ins.

But the Vikings didn't flinch and drafted him, convinced they could bring out Moss's breathtaking talent and believing the off-field issues were behind him. With the addition of Moss, head coach Dennis Green believed he had the team to overtake the Packers.

And in a highly anticipated Monday Night Football showdown at Lambeau Field, the Vikings demonstrated a changing of the guard.

Both teams were 4–0 heading into that game, but when it was over, it was clear the division had a new sheriff in town. In a complete domination of the team that had been to the last two Super Bowls, the Vikings rolled up 545 total yards in a 37–24 win that wasn't as close as it sounded. As well, it ended Green Bay's 25-game home winning streak.

Cunningham torched the Packers for 442 passing yards and four touchdowns, and Moss had his national coming-out party, catching five passes for 190 yards and two scores against the overwhelmed Packers secondary. Carter caught eight passes for 119 yards and Jake Reed added another four receptions for 89 yards and a score.

Meanwhile the Vikings defense bedeviled Favre, intercepting him three times and sacking him twice before he was sent to the sidelines and replaced by backup Doug Pederson.

It was a stunning and dramatic demonstration by Minnesota and the first real sign that the Packers were not the team they had been, even if much of the personnel really had not changed.

And while the Packers did right their ship that season, the signs of stress and dysfunction were starting to creep in. Players privately spoke of how difficult it was to play for Holmgren and how his demands for perfection were starting to wear them down.

And, of course, there was the other elephant in the room—the growing disconnect between Holmgren and Wolf and the head coach's desire (demand?) to have more of a say in personnel decisions.

It was a conflict of Shakespearean proportions, and it played out on the national media stage almost daily.

On one side was Ron Wolf, who had rebuilt the Packers from an NFL joke to a Super Bowl champ and perhaps the most consistent and admired franchise in the league in a matter of five years. A disciple of Oakland Raiders owner/general manager Al Davis, Wolf had worked hard to reach this point in his career and he wasn't about to cede control to anyone unless it was on his terms.

On the other side was Holmgren, perhaps the best offensive mind in the NFL, who had taken the talent presented to him by Wolf and molded it into the best team in the league. Still a young man, he knew there was more to accomplish and he wanted an opportunity to wield the kind of power he believed he had earned.

And while neither man aired his issues in public, it was common knowledge that their relationship had suffered. And it was starting to show on the field.

In a shocking scene during a late-season game at Lambeau Field, the Packers had played an uninspired, mistake-filled first half against the hapless Philadelphia Eagles and trailed 10–6 at halftime.

As players and coaches headed toward the team's tunnel to the locker room, one fan yelled at Holmgren to keep his head in the game and not worry about where he'd be next season. The comment ignited Holmgren's legendary temper and he made his way toward the stands to confront the fan before he was steered away by security personnel.

It was yet another sign that the paint was beginning to peel on the franchise that had spent the previous three seasons on top of professional football.

Despite their season-long problems, the Packers still carved out a solid 11–5 record and claimed the fifth seed in the NFC playoffs. But the powerful Vikings won the NFC Central Division with a 15–1 record, signaling the first time in four years Green Bay did not win the division.

But a rough season could be smoothed over with a strong playoff run and a third straight trip to the Super Bowl, which at that time only one team had accomplished (the AFC's Buffalo Bills, who lost four straight).

And the journey began against a familiar foe in the San Francisco 49ers, a team the Packers had dominated the last few seasons. Indeed, in Holmgren's tenure as head coach, the San Francisco native had beaten his hometown team five times in a row, including three straight in the postseason. As well, Green Bay had beaten the 49ers during the 1998 regular season.

More drama was added to the game as the rumor machine cranked up again. The stories swirling around the Bay Area suggested that 49ers head coach Steve Mariucci, who had previously been an assistant coach in Green Bay under Holmgren and who had tutored Favre in his early years, might be on his way out after just two success-ful seasons. His replacement? Holmgren. And Mariucci would then take over Green Bay.

There was no evidence for any of this, mind you, just juicy talk that added another dimension to what would prove to be an unfor-gettable game.

The Packers and 49ers hammered away at each other on a gorgeous winter afternoon in San Francisco. And when Favre threw a 15-yard touchdown pass to Antonio Freeman with two minutes remaining to give Green Bay a 27–23 lead, it appeared the Packers' hex over the Niners would continue.

But quarterback Steve Young led his offense back the other way in a desperate drive that appeared to end with 37 seconds to play. Young completed a pass to Hall of Fame wide receiver Jerry Rice, who was hit by linebacker Bernardo Harris and safety Scott McGarrahan at the Packers' 43-yard line. As he was going down, Rice fumbled and the ball was scooped up by McGarrahan.

But officials ruled Rice was already down and since there was no replay rule in effect yet, play continued despite vehement protests by both Harris and McGarrahan.

The drive continued and with eight seconds remaining, cornerback Craig Newsome again nearly ended the drive with an interception at the Green Bay 3. But he couldn't hold on to the ball and the Niners had one more chance.

From the 25-yard line, Young dropped back, stumbling as he went, and then found rookie Terrell Owens in the end zone between three Packers defenders. Owens, who had dropped four passes and lost a fumble earlier, was clobbered by Darren Sharper and Harris but held on to the ball for the game-winning score with three seconds left.

On the sideline, Favre and Holmgren just watched stoically as the stadium erupted.

Wolf remembers as well.

"I was in the press box thinking, 'We're on our way to Atlanta [to face the Falcons in the NFC title game] and we have a chance to make it three in a row,'" Wolf said recently. "But it wasn't to be. Jerry Rice fumbled on that last drive and everybody knows it. But there was a rookie official working the game and he shouldn't have been there. But that's the way it was and the next year the NFL brought in instant replay."

Yes, it was over. And in more ways than one.

While the 49ers would lose the following week to the Atlanta Falcons (who would upset the Vikings the week after that before being blown out by Denver in Super Bowl XXXIII), the Packers braced for a turbulent off-season.

And that turbulence wasted no time in descending on Green Bay. Indeed, not even a week after that crushing loss to the 49ers, Holmgren decided it was time to leave the Packers and was named vice president of football operations, general manager, and, of course, head coach of the Seattle Seahawks. He signed an eight-year contract worth at least $4 million a season, making him the highest-paid coach in the NFL. In return, the Packers received a second-round draft pick from the Seahawks (which they used to select cornerback Fred Vinson).

But more than the money, Holmgren was able to coalesce all the power around him. He was in charge of *everything*—much the same way Vince Lombardi had all the control of the Packers in 1959.

Wolf insists there was never any conflict between himself and Holmgren. It was merely the expected by-product brought on by success on the field and, yes, ego.

"I told Mike from the outset that if he had an opportunity to go anywhere that we wouldn't stand in his way," Wolf said. "We wouldn't prevent him from doing it. And when the chance came for him, it resulted in us getting a second-round draft choice."

That loss in San Francisco signaled the quick, though not necessarily unexpected, end to another golden age of Packers football. And while the Packers remained a solid, competitive team over the next decade, three coaches were hired to try to fill the vacuum left by both Wolf (who resigned shortly after the 2000 season) and Holmgren.

Was that one of the most important games in franchise history? Maybe not, but it was certainly close and left many to wonder what might have happened in 1999 if Holmgren had returned. And while it's an intriguing game of "what if?" that's all it will ever be.

Head coaches, in many cases, have shelf lives that they rarely see but players understand all too well. They know that the coaching message begins to lose its edge and the lessons that used to resonate are no longer heard. That was surely the case with Holmgren and the Packers.

But it remains a story of unrealized potential for a team that won one Super Bowl, should have won a second, and may well have reached a third if not for a host of circumstances.

And the frustration of those missed opportunities still lingers.

A Change at the Top
Arizona Cardinals 20, Packers 17
December 2, 2018
If most of the heat and light in the Green Bay Packers organization falls on the starting quarterback, then a close second on that list has to be the head coach.

The head coach of the Green Bay Packers has, at least over the last few decades, had to wear more than a few hats—including public relations coordinator, father figure, and camp counselor who, oh yes, has to know how to put the right players in the right places. It also doesn't hurt if he possesses the personality that can range from game-show host to Darth Vader, sometimes in a matter of seconds.

Over the franchise's more than 100 years of existence, the Packers have had giants as head coaches—Curly Lambeau, Vince Lombardi, and Mike Holmgren—two of whom are in the Pro Football Hall of Fame and a third who probably will be. But as with so many other franchises, they have had their share of misfires as well, such as Dan Devine, Lindy Infante, Ray McLean, Ray Rhodes, Phil Bengtson, Gene Ronzani, Forrest Gregg, and to an extent, Bart Starr.

Sitting somewhere in between is the enigmatic visage of Mike McCarthy, who assumed the role of head coach in 2006 from Mike Sherman, an earnest and well-intentioned man who never quite fit the role of what a Packers head coach should be.

In his nearly 13 years as Green Bay's head coach, McCarthy won a lot of games. In fact, his overall record of 125–77–2 produced a winning percentage of .618, fourth in team history behind the aforementioned giants. His 125 victories are second in team history behind only Lambeau. He led the Packers to nine playoff appearances, including eight in a row at one stage, and in 2010 he dragged an injury-riddled Packers team to their fourth Super Bowl championship.

So the guy could coach.

But to fans, NFL observers, and over time, even some players (who could not quite put a finger on it, fairly or not), McCarthy always seemed about a half-step behind his competition.

The Packers won with superior talent and, often, McCarthy's game plans were brilliant. He was popular with players, great with the fans, and smart. He was everything a Packers head coach should be.

Still, something just wasn't right.

Eventually, it became clear that especially when the playoffs rolled around, the Packers looked unprepared. In 2011, a year after winning the Super Bowl, Green Bay rolled to a 15–1 record and were the clear favorites to reach another championship game. But in their playoff opener against the New York Giants, the Packers were sluggish and tentative and the Giants beat them decisively, 37–20.

And every year after that under McCarthy, some new and bizarre event would pop up to derail Green Bay's latest trek to the championship. There were last-second defeats and overtime collapses, and there were blowouts.

Along the way, McCarthy's coaching was questioned more and more. Whether it was abandoning the running game too soon or playing it too safe on offense, or his puzzling issues with clock management, which cost more than a couple of games, questions were growing about McCarthy's future as head coach.

He had a generational talent at quarterback in Aaron Rodgers, who in his first 10 years as a starter saw Green Bay reach just one Super Bowl.

The storm clouds began to gather on McCarthy in 2017. Due in large measure to Rodgers being lost for most of the season with a broken collarbone, the Packers finished 7–9, their first losing record since 2008, which coincided with the last time they missed the playoffs.

In 2018, however, Rodgers suited up for a full season but did not play up to his usual standard. Still, when their bye week came, the Packers were hanging around with a 3–2–1 record. After the bye, though, the Packers hit the skids, losing four of five heading into a Lambeau Field meeting with the hapless Arizona Cardinals, who had managed to win just 2 of 11 games all season.

In what should have been a walk in the park at home against a bad team, the Packers were awful. They could gain no traction against one of the worst teams in the league, and despite having a clear advantage in personnel, the Packers allowed the Cardinals to hang around and gain confidence.

In the end the Cards took a 20–17 lead with 1:41 left to play on a Zane Gonzalez 41-yard field goal. Rodgers then drove the Packers back downfield, setting up what should have been a 49-yard game-tying field goal from Mason Crosby—which he missed on the final play.

A bad season was getting worse, and for the second straight year Green Bay would miss the playoffs—but this time there would be no excuse with an injured Aaron Rodgers. And it would be the first time since the 2005–2006 seasons that the Packers had missed the postseason in consecutive seasons.

Add to all that the growing rumors that there was conflict between Rodgers and McCarthy on how the offensive game plan was being determined. Stories circulated that Rodgers was ignoring McCarthy's play calls in the huddle and calling the plays he believed would be more effective. And when reporters would ask players the ominous question—"Had McCarthy lost the locker room?"—there were no denials.

The storm clouds had gathered into a full-fledged hurricane.

Afterward, McCarthy was asked about his future with the Packers.

"I mean, I've never been in this spot," McCarthy said in his post-game news conference. "I'm not going to act like I know what the hell I'm going to do tomorrow when they get in here. So, we're going to do what we always do: We're going to represent the Packers the right way, I know that. Other than that, we'll focus on what's in front of us."

It would be only three hours later when McCarthy was summoned to the office of team president Mark Murphy, was thanked for his service to the Packers, and then told those services were no longer needed.

For the first time in franchise history, the Packers had fired a coach during a season, and it sent a thunderbolt through the franchise and through the NFL.

The Packers played out the season under offensive coordinator Joe Philbin as the organization set its sights on perhaps its most important head-coaching hire since Vince Lombardi.

In a process that took barely a month but involved the interviewing of 10 candidates for one of the most sought-after coaching jobs in the NFL, Matt LaFleur, just 39 years old but already with a solid résumé of coaching in the NFL, rose to the top. In the end Murphy and general manager Brian Gutekunst knew they had their man.

"The two things that through all of this have come out is one, his work ethic—he's a grinder. And two, his ability to connect with people—the players, his coaches, personnel staff, people throughout the building," Gutekunst told ESPN's Rob Demovsky. "He's a relentless communicator that way. Those two things have really stood out. This is Matt's first time as a coach, but his ability to stand in front of our team and hold them accountable and set expectations has been impressive."

LaFleur said all the right things at his initial press conference.

"It's always been a dream of mine to be an NFL head coach," he said. "But to be the head coach of the Green Bay Packers, it is surreal and I am extremely humbled. To follow in the footsteps of Vince Lombardi, Mike Holmgren, Mike McCarthy, it's truly an honor."

It was a choice that caught many by surprise and that was questioned by many NFL observers. But a funny thing happened.

In three seasons as the Packers' head coach, LaFleur has led the Packers to three straight division titles and two trips to the NFC Championship Game. His performance has been unmatched by any Packers coach anywhere in history, and that says plenty.

And it came after one of the darker moments in recent team history when a loss to a struggling opponent, at home, seemed to suggest tougher times might be ahead for the Packers.

But, as always seems to be the case, this is a franchise where very little goes as expected.

BACK IN THE BIG TIME
Packers 41, St. Louis Cardinals 16
January 3, 1983

It took a debilitating NFL strike to put the Green Bay Packers back in the postseason after a 10-year absence. But no matter the circumstances, few teams relished the opportunity to continue their season more than the 1982 Packers.

It had been a strange decade that preceded Green Bay's return to the playoffs, starting in 1972, when head coach Dan Devine, who had replaced Vince Lombardi's successor Phil Bengtson in 1971, proceeded to dismantle what was left of those legendary teams of the 1960s for a new cast. His emphasis was on the running game and great defense, and in his second season it all came together with a team that used the running of John Brockington and MacArthur Lane and a solid defense to post a 10–4 record. It was Green Bay's first division title since 1968 and it raised the echoes that, after a brief hiatus, the Packers were back among the NFL's elite.

But a first-round playoff loss to Washington would be the Packers' last appearance in the postseason until 1982. In the meantime, Devine unexpectedly quit the Packers to take over as head coach at the University of Notre Dame after a turbulent 1974 season.

He was replaced by iconic Packers quarterback Bart Starr, who had no head-coaching experience. Over the next seven seasons, the Packers had one winning season and no playoff appearances.

Then came 1982, which was an odd season in its own right. The season started as always, but after two games and no progress in talks between the NFL Players Association and league owners on a range of issues, players walked off the job.

During the strike, fans stewed and complained and vowed never to return to watch pro football. But of course, they did.

As for the striking players who were barred by their teams from even visiting their facilities to work out, many gathered for de facto practices to stay in shape for the time when the strike would end and they'd be recalled.

One of those teams that stayed together for their informal practices were the Packers. And it would make a difference in the long run.

For these Green Bay Packers, absent from the postseason since 1972, this was an opportunity to recapture some of the greatness of the past and build a new foundation of respectability.

By the time the players returned two months later, the schedule was in tatters, and if a playoff system and a Super Bowl were to be held, a new format was needed. The result was a 16-team tournament that would include eight teams from each conference based on season records. To that end, this tournament included two teams with losing records.

The Packers helped themselves immensely by winning their first two games to start the season and then, once the season restarted, going 3–3–1, finishing the "season" 5–3–1 to earn the third seed in the eight-team NFC bracket.

It wasn't perfect, but it was a return to the postseason and Packers fans reveled in it, especially since Green Bay would host its first post-season game since the Ice Bowl in December 1967.

The opponent was the no. 6 seed St. Louis Cardinals, with a 5–4 record and featuring a high-flying offense with quarterback Neil Lomax, running back Ottis Anderson, and wide receiver Roy Green.

But the Packers already had in place the offensive tools that would make them such an entertaining team in 1983—quarterback Lynn

Dickey, wide receivers John Jefferson and James Lofton, tight end Paul Coffman and running back Eddie Lee Ivery.

And that group overwhelmed the Cardinals at Lambeau Field. After falling behind early, 3–0, the Packers scored 28 straight points thanks to three Dickey TD passes to Ivery, Jefferson and Lofton and an Ivery touchdown run.

By halftime Green Bay led 28–9 and the game was all but over.

The Packers went on to spank the Cardinals, 41–16, as Dickey threw for 260 yards and four touchdowns and Jefferson caught six passes for 148 yards and two scores. Meanwhile, the Packers defense, despite giving up 453 yards, forced four turnovers and sacked Lomax five times.

Packers fans rejoiced at the victory by storming the field and tearing down the goalposts. For many fans, it was a return to a glorious past as their Packers, winning their first home playoff game since the Ice Bowl, prepared to reclaim their spot among the NFL hierarchy.

But it was not to be. By beating the Cardinals they would now have to again travel back into their distant past to face the Dallas Cowboys at Texas Stadium. And the results would not be pleasant.

Dickey threw three interceptions, and while the Packers outgained the Cowboys 466 to 375, Dallas made the most of their opportunities to post the 37–26 win.

And while it ended in a way that was not unexpected, it seemed to offer hope that the Packers had, again, turned a corner and would be regular visitors to the postseason.

But it did not happen. In 1983, despite having one of the most entertaining and potent offenses in the NFL, the Packers could not stop anybody on defense. The result was another 8–8 campaign, and after nine disappointing seasons, Bart Starr was finally relieved of his coaching duties.

Ironically, many of his assistant coaches and a number of players believed that Starr had finally found his footing as a head coach and could have turned the Packers' fortunes around.

Even more shocking, as veteran center Larry McCarren said at the time, "Firing Bart Starr as Green Bay's head coach was like firing God."

What followed was another decade of frustration, but for at least a brief time, the Packers were once again back in the spotlight. And it felt like all was right with the world.

An Opportunity Lost

Seattle Seahawks 28, Packers 22
January 18, 2015

It is, after all, just a game. And if your favorite team loses a game, albeit the most important game in the history of the world (as too many fans might imagine), the Earth does not stop spinning, the birds continue to sing, life does in fact go on.

But there are some games. . . .

For Packers fans, this NFC Championship Game might well be the most painful, the most infuriating, the most baffling loss in Green Bay's long postseason history. It came close to making the list of the top 10 most significant games, but it missed out because, in truth, not much changed after the defeat, and because nothing did, perhaps that's the most painful part of the whole scenario.

Put simply, the Packers were within minutes of returning to the Super Bowl. They had flown west and had dominated the favored Seattle Seahawks in perhaps the loudest and most intimidating stadium in the league.

Green Bay had played smart and tough football, forcing five Seattle turnovers, four of them interceptions of passes from quarterback Russell Wilson. The Packers led 16–0 at one point and were still up 19–14 after Seattle scored a seemingly meaningless touchdown with 2:09 left to play.

Everyone knew what would come next. The Seahawks would attempt an onside kick in a vain attempt to gain possession again. Of course, onside kicks in the NFL statistically succeeded almost never, and Green Bay would recover the kick, likely run out the clock, and move on to their sixth Super Bowl. It was so inevitable, in fact, that Seahawks fans had begun streaming to the exits to avoid the inevitable traffic issues.

But it didn't quite work out that way, and the name Brandon Bostick, Green Bay's no. 3 tight end and in the game only because as a receiver he had (supposedly) reliable hands, would find its way into the franchise's hall of infamy.

Seattle kicker Stephen Hauschka did indeed attempt an onside kick and it was a good one. He spun it high in the air, and Bostick, told on the sidelines not to touch the ball and concentrate on his role as a blocker, instead lunged for the ball, stepping in front of sure-handed wide receiver Jordy Nelson, who was set to grab it. The ball bounced off Bostick's helmet and in the mad scramble that ensued, Seattle's Chris Matthews came up with the ball at the 50-yard line.

Stunned and shaken at the turn of events, the Packers defense, which had played so well all day, offered little resistance as the Seahawks rolled 50 yards in just four plays, scoring on a 24-yard run by Marshawn Lynch. The two-point conversion pass, just as Wilson was about to be sacked, gave the Seahawks the shocking 22–19 lead.

It was a collapse worthy of some of the greatest ever seen in American sports, but it wasn't over yet. Aaron Rodgers, playing with a painful calf injury, directed the Packers right back down the field, covering 48 yards in seven plays, and Mason Crosby's 48-yard field goal with 14 seconds remaining tied the game and sent it to overtime.

But inevitability seemed to have set in on this one. The Seahawks won the toss, took the ball, and six plays later won the game when Wilson threw a 35-yard touchdown pass to Jermaine Kearse, who had badly beaten Green Bay cornerback Tramon Williams.

In the morgue-like Packers locker room afterward, there was disbelief, stupefaction, anger, and the realization that they had blown an opportunity that does not come often.

"We kicked their ass up and down the field all day," Packers guard Josh Sitton told the *Milwaukee Journal Sentinel*. "And there's no reason we shouldn't have won the game. Literally 1 of 10 plays you can pick that if we get it, we win the game. It's frustrating when you should have won the game and you're the better team, and I thought we were the better team all day except for three minutes."

Indeed, there were a few plays over the course of the game that caused more than a few puzzled looks. There was poor clock management, odd play calls, poor decisions on and off the field, and, of course, there was Bostick.

"It's been tough," Bostick said to a media horde the next day as the Packers cleaned out their lockers for the season. "I just keep replaying that play in my mind over and over, just trying not to think about it, just trying to get over it. I did my best, but I'll be all right."

Three weeks later, the Packers released Bostick, insisting his blunder had not factored in the decision.

"I think I'm still in shock," Packers wide receiver Randall Cobb said at the time. "I just can't wrap my mind around it. It's going to take some time. This is a rough one to get over."

That loss, and the scope of the opportunity squandered, reverberated among Packers fans and the organization for months. And while the Packers would return to the playoffs the next two seasons, that loss may well have signaled the beginning of the end for head coach Mike McCarthy.

He had taken his place among the best coaches in team history, and in his 13 seasons his 125 victories were second only to Curly Lambeau. His .618 winning percentage was behind only the mighty triumvirate of Lambeau, Vince Lombardi, and Mike Holmgren.

But that loss exposed some real issues in his game management, and over the course of time, players began losing faith in him. High on that list was the most important Packer of all, Aaron Rodgers.

Green Bay missed the playoffs in 2017, and 12 games into a quickly unraveling 2018 season, the Packers organization did what they had never done before—dismissed a head coach during the season.

And while it's difficult to pin all of this on Bostick's blunder, that play and that game started a ball rolling downhill that, fortunately for the Packers, stopped at the feet of one Matt LaFleur.

SOME COLD REALITY
New York Giants 23, Packers 20
January 20, 2008

This game finds itself on the list for a simple reason: it was Brett Favre's last as Green Bay's quarterback and his last play, perhaps to the surprise of no one, was an interception.

Was this as painful a playoff loss as the one in Seattle? Probably not and only because of the circumstances.

But it was another NFC Championship Game, and this one was played at Lambeau Field and in the kind of frigid weather conditions that should have played right into Green Bay's hands.

The temperature at game time was minus-1 and fell to minus-5 by the end, but it was the Packers who seemed frozen in place most of the game. Brett Favre did throw two touchdown passes, including a scintillating 90-yarder to Donald Driver, the longest playoff score in team history.

But for much of the night, the Giants, who came in as the sixth (and last) seed in the NFC playoffs, outplayed the second-seeded Packers, who were making their first trip to the NFC title game in 10 years.

New York had already beaten the Tampa Bay Buccaneers and top-seeded Dallas Cowboys with a combination of great defense and just enough offense to get the job done. This game would be no different.

The Giants held the Packers to 264 total yards and intercepted Favre twice—he never looked comfortable the entire game.

Still, even though the Packers seemed stuck in neutral, they had managed to get the game into overtime, thanks to two missed field goals by New York's Lawrence Tynes.

And in the extra session the Packers got the ball first. But it ended badly, and quickly. On third down Favre attempted to throw a relatively safe sideline pass to Driver, but the ball was thrown poorly and Giants cornerback Corey Webster stepped in front to intercept at the Green Bay 38.

Four plays later Tynes found his redemption by nailing the 47-yard field goal to seal the victory for the upstart Giants, who may well have been the NFL's team of destiny, as two weeks later they would stun the unbeaten and heavily favored New England Patriots to win Super Bowl XLII.

It was not a great performance by Favre, who completed just 19 of 35 passes for 236 yards, with 90 coming on the TD catch and run by Driver.

Favre reflected afterward, "For me, I kept thinking how many more opportunities are we going to let slip away?"

As it turned out, the answer was none.

Whether that game pushed Favre to his limits or whether he'd already had it in his mind, a month later the greatest quarterback in team history (to that point, at least) tearfully announced his retirement.

It was a stunning announcement in one way because Favre was still playing at a high level and he knew he was still with a team that had the personnel to make a championship run.

But in another way it was Favre being Favre. He had teased and toyed with the front office and Packers fans for three years about his desire to retire. Indeed, one off-season the rumors were so prevalent that Favre was walking away, Wisconsin media descended on his Mississippi compound to see what was happening. As it turned out, absolutely nothing was happening. It was, one more time, Favre being Favre.

But in March 2008 before a packed auditorium, in a rambling but poignant event, the man who had been the quarterback for nearly an entire generation of Packers fans was calling it quits.

And though he spoke a lot on a lot of topics, the main point seemed to be when he said, "I know I can still play. I'm just not sure I want to."

It was a statement full of landmines and potholes, and more than a few witnesses on hand doubted Favre would follow through.

They were right, and the next five months would provide the kind of drama, angst, uncertainty, anger, and bewilderment that the franchise had rarely seen.

It was time for a new direction, and the quarterback job now belonged to Aaron Rodgers.

INTRODUCING THE FUTURE
Packers 24, Minnesota Vikings 19
September 8, 2008

Eight months earlier, the Green Bay Packers had last made an appearance at frozen Lambeau Field and the results were disappointing.

Facing a New York Giants team that had barely slipped into the playoffs, the Packers played tentatively and without passion and were beaten in overtime, 23–20. Worse, the man they had come to rely on to deliver the goods, quarterback Brett Favre, had played poorly, including throwing a horrible interception in the overtime that set up the Giants' game-winning field goal.

But as had become a habit for Packers fans, there was a sad shake of the head, a resigned shrug of the shoulders, and then the comforting thought that there was always next season because, with Brett Favre at the helm, there was always the promise of great things.

Now, eight months later, everything had changed.

After a bitter off-season of recriminations, accusations, the occasional threat, and frequent childish misunderstandings, as the 2009 season opened, Favre was no longer the Packers' starting quarterback. He wasn't even the backup quarterback. Indeed, he wasn't a Packer at all, and it was a sight and a feeling no one could quite get their head around.

But the Packers organization had done what it felt it needed to do after Favre had announced his retirement in March. They had moved on as they needed and perhaps wanted to do, and Aaron Rodgers was now the quarterback after a three-year apprenticeship behind Favre.

That Favre had changed his mind and wanted to return to the role he had held for a mind-blowing 16 seasons did not impact a front office convinced it was time for a new direction.

It was a nasty, confusing period as Favre tried to negotiate with general manager Ted Thompson and coach Mike McCarthy regarding his future with Green Bay. It was a scene unworthy of a future Hall of Famer who had meant so much to the franchise. But now, he appeared to be begging to be brought back and the Packers brass appeared unfeeling and tone-deaf. It was a bad look for all involved.

In the end, of course, the Packers traded Favre to the New York Jets for a fourth-round draft pick and set their sights on a new, untested quarterback.

Aaron Rodgers actually was unveiled to the home fans in the preseason opener against the Cincinnati Bengals while Favre was still hoping to reclaim his starting job.

So when Rodgers ran on the field, boos filtered through Lambeau. But he played well in a limited appearance and seemed to tune out the maelstrom around him to show a glimpse of the mental toughness that would be so valuable for him in the years to come.

But this was the regular season now, against the division-nemesis Vikings, and with Favre officially and finally gone, Rodgers had to show a dubious and spoiled fan base that he was a worthy successor to the throne.

He wasted little time. On his first play he completed a simple seven-yard pass to tight end Donald Lee and he would go from there.

His first TD pass (as the starter) was a one-yard toss to fullback Korey Hall. Of course, Rodgers' first TD pass as a pro came the year before in a national Thursday night loss to the Dallas Cowboys when Rodgers came on in the second quarter to replace Favre, who had injured his elbow. In that relief appearance, Rodgers proved to Favre (and McCarthy) that he could be a no. 1 quarterback when he completed 18 of 26 passes for 201 yards, no interceptions, and an 11-yard TD strike to Greg Jennings.

Against the Vikings, Rodgers was methodical, smart, and controlled. He was the anti-Favre, whose reputation as a "gunslinger" Favre had grown to love and nurture and had led to head-scratching plays and far too many interceptions (he still holds the NFL record with 336, of which 286 came with the Packers). But Rodgers took few chances, was technically far more proficient than Favre, knew where he wanted to throw the ball, and had the touch, skill, and presence of mind to put it where it needed to be.

All those skills were on display against Minnesota, which was expected to overtake Green Bay that season at the top of the division.

Rodgers completed 18 of 22 passes for 178 yards and one touchdown. He also ran for 35 yards and scored on a 1-yard sneak, capping it with his first effort at a Lambeau Leap that he has rarely tried since.

It was a crucial and noteworthy performance as Rodgers looked to assume a role that would have been difficult for any quarterback to take over. But he had made his first statement that the quarterback job in Green Bay, one of the most noteworthy positions in the NFL, was in good hands.

"Aaron managed the game," head coach Mike McCarthy told the *Milwaukee Journal Sentinel* afterward. "Not taking chances. Play to the play call. Taking what the defense gives you. I was pleased."

Teammates were as well.

"People need to get behind him," veteran left tackle Chad Clifton told the *Journal Sentinel*. "He's a good football player. You would have thought he was a 10-year veteran tonight. He was very calm, very collected. He played an outstanding game."

Even the Vikings were impressed.

"I thought it was going to be easier playing against Rodgers than Favre," defensive end Jared Allen told the *Journal Sentinel*. "But it was easier playing Favre [last year] because he was not as mobile. Rodgers froze the defensive linemen with the play-action and his movement."

And for Rodgers, the opportunity to finally prove himself was truly special.

"I've been dreaming about this for four years," he said afterward.

And so, officially and finally, another new era in Packers football had begun, and while the hangover left from Favre remained (and still remains in some cases), Rodgers would show he was a quarterback who could take the position in new and different places in Green Bay.

He threw for more than 4,000 yards that season with 28 touchdown passes and 13 interceptions. But the most important number was six, the amount of wins Green Bay compiled that season. With Favre under center, Green Bay suffered just one losing season, and in the final analysis, that would be the ultimate barometer for a dubious fan base.

Nonetheless, Aaron Rodgers had made his mark that night, and unknown to all those who watched, he had begun his journey as the best quarterback in team history.

MONDAY NIGHT MANIA
Packers 48, Washington Redskins 47
October 17, 1983

The next game on our list was not one of the most important in franchise history. It did not alter standings or lead to a Super Bowl or a new era of winning. It did not produce a great player or an unforgettable play.

But aside from Super Bowls, championship games, and of course, the Ice Bowl, it may be the most memorable game in franchise history. It may not have been one of the most important games, but it may have been the most fun, so it finds its way onto our list for that reason alone.

Remember?

For the Green Bay Packers, the previous 15 years had not been kind to them. Since their last NFL championship in 1967 and with the gradual and relentless dismantling of the 1960s juggernaut, the Packers had fallen back into irrelevance, not unlike the place they inhabited in the late 1940s and 1950s.

In the 15 seasons since Vince Lombardi was carried off the Orange Bowl field by his grateful players in Super Bowl II, the Packers had managed just four (barely) winning seasons and two trips to the playoffs.

Hope would always bloom with each new season, but even with the iconic Bart Starr as head coach, nothing was changing. The Packers, at best, were an average NFL team. And there was no Vince Lombardi waiting in the wings waiting to deliver them.

Still in 1983, with an exciting and potent offense under veteran offensive coordinator Bob Schnelker, the Packers were at least fun to watch. As well, the strike-shortened 1982 season had produced a 5–3–1 record and a playoff victory (their first since 1968), so there was optimism—albeit tentative.

Intrigued by their potential, the NFL gave the Packers a slot on the coveted *Monday Night Football* schedule—and at Lambeau Field no less—only the second time *MNF* had been to Lambeau Field since the series started in 1970.

The opponent? The defending Super Bowl champion Washington Redskins, who were 5–1 and riding a five-game winning streak in which they had dismantled everyone they'd played.

It was believed the Redskins defense would throttle quarterback Lynn Dickey and his offensive weapons, which included wide receivers James Lofton and John Jefferson and tight end Paul Coffman.

And the Packers defense? Ugh. The joke at the time was the Packers offense had to be high-scoring just to counteract all the points allowed by the defense.

"Yeah, we weren't very good," Dickey recalled years later.

What resulted was a game that, for pure entertainment value, may never be topped at Lambeau Field.

Another great story was one told by center Larry McCarren, now a longtime fixture on Green Bay TV and the Packers' radio network color analyst, but back then was known as "Rock" for his endurance and toughness.

"Bob Schnelker told us before the game, 'To hell with the defense. We're going to throw everything at the Redskins,'" McCarren recalled. "He said, 'We're going to have fun.'"

Did they ever.

The Packers brought out every play in their arsenal, from halfback options to plays seemingly drawn up on the sideline on the spot, to keep Washington's defense off-balance.

"It was not a good night to be a defensive back," said Mark Murphy, the current Packers president, who back then was a highly regarded safety for the Redskins but who that night was under constant assault.

In the book *Game of My Life*, Packers quarterback Lynn Dickey recalled that it was a night that seemed special from the beginning.

"In warmups for that game, it seemed the ball was just spinning," he said. "I can't explain it. Some days you can just tell in warmups that it's going to be a good day. And during the game I couldn't throw a wobbly pass if I tried."

And it continued throughout the game as everything seemed to fall into place.

"I was getting great protection and [Washington] was getting no rush on me whatsoever," he said. "It was like shooting fish in a barrel in the first half."

But what several Packers also remember is how head coach Bart Starr approached the game.

The normally stoic Starr, who guarded his emotions closely, was in his ninth season as head coach and many believed that, finally, after taking over the team in 1975 with no coaching experience of any kind that he was finally evolving into a quality head coach.

As the Redskins game approached, players could sense Starr was annoyed when a Washington player (believed to be tight end Don Warren) told a Washington TV reporter that the game against Green Bay would be a "rout."

"He didn't let things get under his skin often, but that did," Dickey recalled in the book. "On the night of the game we went out for warm-ups and came back in, and before we were ready to come back out he put that quote back up on the overhead projector. He said, 'This is what these guys think of you.' He also said, 'It's going to be a rout,' but he added, 'He didn't say which way.' We thought that was kind of cool. It was a little extra pump for us."

Perhaps, but as much as the players respected and liked Starr, time and numbers were working against him. In his previous eight years Green Bay had made one playoff appearance and produced just two winning seasons, and the thought among observers was that if Starr was going to make it to a 10th season, he'd need to take his team back to the postseason.

He certainly had assembled an offense that could get there. What would stop them was a dreadful defense that would give up an average of 377 yards and 27 points per game that season.

So two high-powered offenses collided on that chilly October and the result was a *Monday Night Football* game still remembered years later.

Ironically, the night got started with the Packers' much-maligned defense making a key play when linebacker Mike Douglass scooped up a Joe Washington fumble and returned it 22 yards for the first touchdown. It only got more interesting after that as the two teams traded haymakers.

"It was just a fun game," Dickey said. "I don't remember the score at halftime [Green Bay led 24–20] but toward the end of the third quarter, Bob Schnelker looked at me on the sidelines and elbowed me and said, 'Keep plugging away. They can't stop us.' He said that we may have to score 40 points to win this game and, looking back, we probably should have lost the game."

As the points piled up and the clock wound down, it seemed fairly obvious that the old cliché would come true—the team with the ball last would win.

A 20-yard Jan Stenerud field goal with 54 seconds remaining gave the Packers a 48–47 lead, but that was more than enough time for the Redskins to score again. Indeed, Washington roared back to drive 55 yards to the Green Bay 22 to set up a game-winning 39-yard field goal.

"Joe Theismann did such a great job leading them right back down the field and I'm thinking, 'Oh my God, we scored 48 points and we're going to lose this thing.'"

But Redskins kicker Mark Moseley, who had already drilled four field goals that night, missed the kick, sending the Lambeau Field crowd into a frenzy.

Theismann, Moseley's longtime holder, recalled later that he looked at his kicker and shook his head.

"You've got to be kidding me," he said.

The Redskins rolled up 552 total yards while the Packers amassed 473 yards. Dickey was superb, completing 22 of 31 passes for 387 yards and three touchdowns.

"I remember [Redskins fullback] John Riggins came up to me after the game and the first thing out of his mouth was, 'Some rout, huh?'" Dickey recalled. "It was just a wild and crazy night. Sometimes they happen when you least expect it. But it was Lambeau Field and people were having fun. And it was a lot of fun."

What many players remember from that night was the raucous, celebratory air after the game, as fans, so unaccustomed to such a special victory, refused to go home, anxious to soak up what they knew was a night never to be repeated.

"It was, comparatively speaking, a very memorable moment in Packers history," center Larry McCarren said in the book *Game of My Life*. "It was a good opponent and it was on Monday night and I remember how good it felt to walk off the field as winners."

The final score was a *Monday Night Football* record that lasted until 2018 when the Los Angeles Rams beat the Kansas City Chiefs 54–51.

That October 1983 game would also prove to be the highlight of the Packers season, as over the remaining nine games Green Bay would lose five, including three in overtime.

It was another 8–8 record, another taste of mediocrity, and another missed opportunity. And after nine seasons, Starr was finally relieved of his head-coaching duties.

But for one night, Green Bay was once again the center of the NFL universe—a place in which it would not return for more than a decade.

THE BEGINNING OF THE END?
San Francisco 49ers 13, Packers 10
January 22, 2022

Due to the vagaries of time and deadlines and the sometimes glacial pace of decision-making by those for whom the decisions matter most, the answer as to where, or even if, this game ends up on the list of the franchise's most important must remain unanswered for now.

But the thought among many, viewed in the cold light of reality, is that the Packers' stunning loss to the 49ers could provide a seismic shift in the future of the franchise.

"I didn't expect this," said a downcast Aaron Rodgers after Green Bay fell to the upstart Niners in the snow, freezing temperatures, and sell-out crowd at Lambeau Field.

Few did. After all, the Packers had just finished another superb regular season under third-year coach Matt LaFleur. Despite an off-season filled with uncertainty and drama and anger, mostly generated by the seemingly unhappy but mostly bemused Rodgers, the Packers took their place as the NFL's betting favorite to win the Super Bowl.

Despite a raft of injuries that sidelined many of the team's top starters at one time or another, Green Bay still posted a 13–4 record, earned the NFC's top seed and a first-round playoff bye and, in what was supposed to be the biggest advantage, they would hold home-field advantage in perhaps the NFL's top homefield venue.

Leading the way, of course, was Rodgers, who had made himself one of the league's top unending stories and lightning rods all season.

It began with a leaked media report that Rodgers was unhappy, especially with general manager Brian Gutekunst and his seeming disinterest in keeping resources on the team that Rodgers wanted and needed. It didn't help that in the NFL draft the year before, Gutekunst had traded up to select Utah State quarterback Jordan Love in the first round as the seeming heir apparent to Rodgers. That pick had surprised Rodgers, and though he insisted he had no ill will toward the new guy, he seethed at Gutekunst and what he saw as the overt disrespect shown to the veteran quarterback.

It was, once again, the Brett Favre drama from years earlier that Rodgers had reluctantly found himself in the middle of, and he wanted no part in it.

So it was an off-season of veiled threats and snarky hints and shrugged shoulders as Rodgers decided whether, first, he even wanted to play football again and, second, if he wanted to play in Green Bay.

This drama enveloped not only the organization but Packers fans, NFL officials, and the national media. What would Rodgers do? Was he playing a game in an effort to force a trade? Was he simply Aaron Rodgers being Aaron Rodgers? No one knew. But Rodgers knew that since the April before the season began, everyone was living in his world.

As training camp neared, though, the Packers restructured his contract, providing him an out after the 2022 season if he wanted it, and Gutekunst went back and re-signed several of Rodgers's favorite players, such as wide receiver Randall Cobb.

But Rodgers wasn't finished tweaking the establishment. As the COVID-19 pandemic continued to rage during the season, Rodgers tested positive just prior to an important game with the Kansas City Chiefs, a game he would be forced to miss due to NFL testing protocol.

Rodgers insisted he had been "inoculated" for the virus but admitted he had not been vaccinated due to what he said was a bad reaction to one of the vaccine's ingredients. Rogers was roundly barbecued by the media, vaccine proponents, ex-players, and even some politicians. Railing against a "woke" American mentality, Rodgers stood his ground and, even through the withering criticism, he kept his bemused smile.

Through it all, though, Rodgers had another football season for the ages and his teammates happily latched on for the ride.

Rodgers again threw for more than 4,000, despite missing a game and playing the last half of the season with a broken pinkie toe he suffered while working out during his COVID isolation. He threw 37 touchdown passes and just four interceptions, two of which came in the season opener.

He was as good as he had ever been at age 38 and his performance secured a fourth NFL MVP award and his second in a row.

Which was why the stunning first-round loss, the fourth postseason setback suffered by the Packers to the 49ers in the past eight seasons, was such a surprise. It was supposed to be different this season, especially with seemingly every aspect of the team coming together—from the return of key injured players to home-field advantage to improved play of the defense to the force that was Rodgers.

But the one aspect of the Packers that had not improved was special teams and, in the end, that's what cost them a shot at a Super Bowl. A blocked punt was returned for a late touchdown; a field goal was blocked; a long kickoff return set up another 49ers score.

And when Niners' kicker Robbie Gould drilled a field goal on the last play of the game, Rodgers could do nothing but look skyward as the snow fell.

In truth, as Rodgers said, he had not played well either, held without a postseason touchdown pass for the first time since the 2010 NFC title game, which the Packers won.

"I definitely take my share of the blame," he told the media.

But now the questions begin again. And Packers fans may not like the answers.

In a 17-minute postgame press conference, Rodgers spoke of his love of the Packers, his teammates, and the fans. He said his relationship with Gutekunst had improved considerably and that he would have some tough decisions to make.

"There's a lot of players whose futures are up in the air, so it definitely will be interesting to see which way some of those decisions will go," Rodgers said. "But I'll have the conversations with Brian in the next week or so and get a little bit more clarity and think about my own future and how much longer I want to keep doing this."

And as Rodgers walked off the snowy, silent Lambeau Field after another crushing season-ending disappointment, the questions immediately rose back to the surface about whether this had been his final game for this iconic franchise.

Over the previous year he had dropped enough hints to sink a battleship that this could, or maybe not, be it for him in Green Bay. And after this loss, coming at the end of a superb season in which all the signs had lined up to seemingly suggest a second Super Bowl title may be at hand, this loss suggested to many that enough was enough for the enigmatic quarterback.

But in early March, Rodgers, just a few weeks after earning his fourth NFL MVP honor (and second straight), tweeted that he would indeed return to the Packers for the 2022 season. Soon after that he made it official, signing a new three-year deal worth roughly $150 million.

Though this guarantees nothing for Rodgers or the Packers, it was a good sign. Of course, while he remains a quarterback operating at high level, the offseason was not kind to the Packers. All-Pro record-setting wide receiver Davante Adams was traded to the Las Vegas Raiders, and the speedy downfield threat, Marcus Valdes-Scantling, signed with the Kansas City Chiefs.

Now Rodgers will start again with a new cast and, again, questions will be raised about where the Packers go. But if nothing else has been learned in his nearly two decades with this team, the evidence is undeniable that those who underestimate Rodgers do so at their own risk.

ACKNOWLEDGMENTS

THIS IS THE 15TH BOOK I'VE WRITTEN ABOUT THE GREEN BAY PACK-
ers and the players who have been a part of this unusual and remarkable
franchise.

And what has always stood out for me is the passion, the pride, and,
yes, the frustration and perhaps some envy of what has been accomplished by this franchise. It's really a remarkable narrative, one that has
been retold and burnished over the decades. It's a story that cannot be
told any longer in the world of modern sports because, quite simply, a
small city in northeast Wisconsin (or anywhere else for that matter)
could not form a professional football team that would survive and
thrive, and fail and succeed, and still carve out a place in the American
sports landscape.

What has made it even remarkable from my perspective is that
through all those adjectives and verbs and hyperbole written over the
years, there has always been something new and different to write
about. That has made this journey fun and enriching and, even now, a
little surprising.

I started on this path in 1993, when I assisted a fellow writer on a
book celebrating the 75th anniversary of the team. It was a very different time then, a very different team, and very different circumstances
all those years ago.

Back then the Packers were pinning their hopes on an untested but
promising young quarterback, a new coach with an ambitious plan, and
a no-nonsense general manager who knew what he wanted and would
do just about anything to make it happen.

Brett Favre, that intriguing young quarterback, had shown flashes
of true brilliance in the 1992 season when he stepped in for an injured

Don Majkowski and led the Packers to a last-second victory over the Cincinnati Bengals. The game was played at Lambeau Field in front of what now was a crowd of around 12 million. That's because, to hear them tell it, *every* Packers fan was at the game and sitting on the 50-yard line, watching this untamed kid fling footballs everywhere, uninterested and unconcerned that he wasn't even following the game plan.

The young and also untested head coach, Mike Holmgren, recalled at the time, "He was calling formations that we didn't even have."

He smiled when he said it, but he really wasn't all that amused by what he had seen.

And the general manager, Ron Wolf, had moved boldly since accepting the role near the end of a disastrous 1991 season, a position many of his friends in pro football had told him to turn down.

"But I liked the challenge," he said at the time.

He was down on the sideline toward the end of Favre's dramatic coming-out party, and he knew then—in ways he could never really articulate when he gave up a first-round draft pick to acquire Favre from the disinterested Atlanta Falcons—that the Packers would be headed in a new direction.

And while every Green Bay fan obviously wasn't there in person to watch this remarkable sight, what each of them did know was that, after some 20 years of stultifying mediocrity, the Packers might just be on the way back. And this kid, and this coach, could be the reasons why.

Yes, Brett Favre soon figured out just about everything, and over the next two decades he would become one of the game's best, most entertaining, most infuriating, and most unforgettable players. The Packers would win one Super Bowl, nearly win a second, and take their place among the elite and consistently successful franchises in the NFL.

And Packers fans would go along for the ride with a cast of characters over the years that included players like Reggie White, LeRoy Butler, Donald Driver, Aaron Rodgers, Desmond Howard, Robert Brooks, Ahman Green, Clay Matthews, Charles Woodson, Greg Jennings, Davante Adams, and so many others.

When I first started these Packers projects, I had no idea where they would lead me. First as a Packers beat writer, then a columnist, and then an interested observer, I had watched this organization take steps forward, back, and sideways.

Of course it has never been a linear path; nothing that interesting can ever be. But for every gut-wrenching, season-ending defeat, there has been an Antonio Freeman plucking a ball off his thigh and turning it into a touchdown on a rainy Monday night against the Vikings.

It has continued in fits and starts with such events, following the selection of a quarterback in 2005 who at one time had been the top QB in the NFL Draft but had unbelievably dropped to no. 24, where the stunned Packers happily picked him.

The rest, as said way too often, is history. By 2021 Aaron Rodgers had served as the Packers' longest-running quarterback, surpassing his predecessor Brett Favre.

There has been another Super Bowl championship under Rodgers and several gut-wrenching near-misses (Brandon Bostick, anybody?). There has been controversy and tragedy and bad football and really good football and everything in between.

For the first time in franchise history, the Packers fired a head coach during a season, and for four months prior to the start of the 2021 slate, Rodgers kept all of Wisconsin, Packers fans everywhere, and the NFL in a state of freaked-out uncertainty as he decided whether he even wanted to play for the Packers again.

Great Packers have died, and the list could populate a hall of fame: Bart Starr, Jim Taylor, Paul Hornung, Willie Davis, Reggie White, Wayne Simmons, Herb Adderley, and Willie Wood.

It has been my arduous but most pleasant task to compile a list of the games that I, assisted by a list of Packers experts, believe check all of the boxes as the most pivotal in team history.

Yes, it's another book on the Green Bay Packers. But this is a franchise that seems to make news because of its long, distinguished history and that has included the type of characters that would find a place in any writer's dream scenario.

I would like to thank Niels Aaboe, senior editor at Globe Pequot/Lyons Press, for his assistance on this book. He and I have worked together on a number of projects, and he has always been a pro who has provided support and insight and, most important, the opportunity to continue writing about this unique American sports franchise.

And this project would have gone nowhere rapidly without the memories and expertise of Cliff Christl, the Packers' team historian, who grew up in Green Bay and had the joyful, and daunting, task of writing about his hometown team as a member of the *Milwaukee Journal*. There has been no better writer about the Packers and there has been no one more accomplished as the team's historian. His advice was invaluable.

I'd also like to thank John Perney, my former colleague at Albion College in Michigan, where we worked together in the communications office. On short notice, he agreed to edit the final rendition of this project and once again reinforced what I have told everyone else—he's the best editor around—and I am immensely grateful.

Finally, I'd like to thank former Packers general manager Ron Wolf, who indulged me and answered patiently and expansively a lot of the same questions he has answered a hundred times over the years (and hopefully a few he has never been asked). I was fortunate to be writing about the Packers when Wolf got his start in Green Bay, and during his career and in his retirement he has been a constant source of assistance. I have enjoyed our conversations.

SOURCE NOTES

I AM GRATEFUL TO GREEN BAY PACKERS HISTORIAN CLIFF CHRISTL for his assistance with this book, especially with information regarding the Packers' formative early years. I have also relied on information available online from *Sports Illustrated*, the *Milwaukee Journal Sentinel*, the *Green Bay Press-Gazette*, and Packers.com.

I have used information from books I have previously written on the Packers, which are listed here:

Facing the Green Bay Packers. New York: Sports Publishing, 2016.

Game of My Life: Memorable Stories of Packers Football. Champaign, IL: Sports Publishing, 2004.

The Green Bay Packers All-Time All-Stars: The Best Players in Each Position for the Green and Gold. Guilford, CT: Lyons Press, 2019.

Green Bay Packers: Where Have You Gone? New York: Sports Publishing, 2015.

Green Bay Packers: Yesterday & Today. Lincolnwood, IL: Publications International, 2009.

Ice Bowl '67: The Packers, the Cowboys and the Game That Changed the NFL. New York: Sports Publishing, 2017.

Tales from the Green Bay Packers Sideline. New York: Sports Publishing, 2015.

Titletown Again: The Super Bowl Season of the 1996 Green Bay Packers, Boulder, CO: Taylor Trade Publishing, 1997.

Other sources include:

Favre, Brett, with Chris Havel. *Favre: For the Record*. New York: Doubleday, 1997.

Hornung, Paul, with Chuck Carlson. *The Paul Hornung Scrapbook*. Chicago: Triumph, 2014.

Kramer, Jerry. *Jerry Kramer's Inside the Locker Room: The Lost Tapes of His 1967 Championship Season* (audio CD). Krammer and Company, 2005.

All other sourcing has been credited in the book when needed.

INDEX

Brooks, Robert, 101, 105
Brown, Ed, 29, 52
Brown, Gilbert, 129
Brown, Roger, 40
Brown, Tom, 57, 61–62, 67
Brunell, Mark, 129, 144
Buck, Jack, 98
Buckley, Curtis, 123
Butler, LeRoy, 102, 105, 110, 134, 136–37

Cade, Mossy, 87
Caffey, Lee Roy, 49, 78
Calhoun, George Whitney, 4, 23, 166
Campen, James, 95
Carolina Panthers, vii, 115, 124–26, 128
Carpenter, Lew, 27–28
Carr, Joe, 13
Chandler, Don, 77
Chicago Bears
  1963 season, 48
  2010 Packers vs., 157, 159–161
  Halas, George, 6, 24–25
  Howard's punt return against, 121
  as perennial Packers rival, 6, 21, 39–40, 87, 117, 159
  Portsmouth Spartans vs., 12–13
  season opener game, 28–29, 50
  Western Division assignment, 13

Chicago Cardinals, 5, 13, 23, 28, 51. *See also* Arizona Cardinals; St. Louis Cardinals
Childress, Brad, 149
Chmura, Mark, 101, 108, 120, 124
Christl, Cliff, 5–8, 35–36, 38–40, 60
Cincinnati Bengals, 94–95, 187, 198
Cincinnati Reds, 13
City Stadium, 16, 28, 38, 50–51. *See also* Lambeau Field
Clark, Frank, 56
Clay, Willie, 131
Cleveland Browns, xi, 27–28, 52–53, 62
Cleveland Indians, 11, 12
Clifton, Chad, 188
Cobb, Randall, 183, 194
Coffman, Paul, 179–180, 190
Collins, Kerry, 125
Collins, Nick, 162
Collins, Todd, 160–61
Comp, Irv, 21, 22
COVID-19 pandemic, 194–95
Cowboys-Packers rivalry, 125
Crosby, Mason, 163, 176, 182
Cunningham, Randall, 170
Cuozzo, Gary, 52
Currie, Dan, 25, 39
Cutler, Jay, 157, 160

opening game team speech, 25
Packers second dynasty and,
   168
passing of, 81
picking his successor, 79
playoffs as spark for, 60–61
Starr and, xii–xiii, 25
stepping down as head coach,
   79, 86
at Super Bowl II, 76–78
trading with New York Giants,
   28
as untested head coach, xii
wanting back-to-back
   championships, 53
as Washington Redskins head
   coach, 81
Lombardi Avenue, 51–52
Los Angeles Raiders, 97, 117.
   See also Las Vegas Raiders;
   Oakland Raiders
Los Angeles Rams, 30, 52, 60,
   104, 193
Love, Jordan, 194
Lynch, Marshawn, 182

Madden, John, 92
Majkowski, Don, 89, 94
Mangini, Eric, 147
Mara, Wellington, 42
Mariucci, Steve, 97, 172
Marshall, George Preston, 14
Martin, Curtis, 131
Mathis, Terrance, 105
Matte, Tom, 52–53

Matthews, Chris, 182
McCarren, Larry, 180, 190, 193
McCarthy, Mike
   firing of, 177
   game-management skills, 155,
      175–77
   on heading to the Super Bowl,
      161
   on losing to Favre's Vikings,
      150
   overall record, 175
   on replacing Favre, 146
   Rodgers and, 176–77, 183, 188
   on role of head coach, 175
   at Super Bowl XLV, 162, 164
McCrary, Herdis, 6
McDonald, Tommy, xiii
McGarrahan, Scott, 172
McGee, Max, xii, 25, 27, 28–29
McHan, Lamar, 28–29
McLean, Ray, xiii, 24, 26
McNally, Johnny "Blood," 4–5, 6
Mendenhall, Rashard, 162
Menninger Clinic, 119
Mercein, Chuck, 62, 68–69, 77
Meredith, Don, 56–57, 63, 67
Metcalf, Eric, 105
Miami Dolphins, 133, 156
Michalske, Mike, 4–5
Mills, Sam, 125
Minneapolis Marines, 165–67
Minneapolis Red Jackets, 11
Minnesota Vikings
   1964 season, 50
   1991 Packers vs., 92

ABOUT THE AUTHOR

Chuck Carlson is an award-winning journalist who has written numerous sports books on subjects ranging from golf to baseball. But his main focus had been on the players and history of the Green Bay Packers, having written on quarterback Brett Favre, Green Bay's two most recent Super Bowl titles, the 1967 "Ice Bowl," the best players at each position in team history and more. He is a frequent freelance writer and has written for newspapers in Virginia, Maryland, Nevada, Washington, Illinois, and Wisconsin. He lives in Marshall, Michigan.